The Planetary Gestures in Eurythmy

The Planetary Gestures in Eurythmy

Werner Barfod

Floris Books

Translated by Sally Lake-Edwards

First published in German as *Planetengebärden und Menschenwesen* by Verlag am Goetheanum, Dornach in 2009. First published in English by Floris Books, Edinburgh in 2025

© 2009 Verlag am Goetheanum
English version © 2025 Floris Books

Werner Barfod has asserted his right under the Copyright, Designs and Patent Act 1988 to be identified as the Author of this Work
All rights reserved. No part of this book may be reproduced in any form without written permission of Floris Books, Edinburgh
www.florisbooks.co.uk

 Also available as an eBook

Authorised EU Representative: Easy Access System Europe, Mustamae tee 50, 10621 Tallinn, Estonia
gpsr.requests@easproject.com
British Library CIP Data available
ISBN 978-178250-941-7

Contents

Preface	9

Part I

1. Forming the Eurythmy Gestures for the Planets	13
An overview of the seven gestures	13
The seven gestures individually	14
The human being: both centre and sphere in the gestures	19
2. The Characteristics of the Planetary Gestures	21
3. The Seven Attitudes of the I in the Soul	23
The dual form of the human members	23
The seven faculties of the I in the soul	24
4. The I as a Being of Breath	26
The I manifested in twelvefold, sevenfold and threefold form	26
The rhythm of the I reflected in the members	26
The archetypal gesture of contraction and expansion	27
5. Planetary Influences in Prenatal and Earthly Existence	28
Human abilities as a reflection of prenatal lunar forces	28
The seven life processes of the natural and 'cultural' etheric	29
The planetary forces in Rudolf Steiner's Ephesus verse	31
The seven life processes as the working of the etheric body	32
Seven steps for practising eurythmy	32
6. The Planetary Processes in Varying Sequences	34
The sequence working in the etheric body	34
The path to earth in the Moon sphere	34
The planetary sequence in Rudolf Steiner's Twelve Moods	35
The planetary sequence in evolution	37
7. The Seven Vowel Responses of the Etheric Body	38

8. The Seven Levels of Manifestation of the Vowels — 41
   - A *in seven stages* — 42
   - E *in seven stages* — 43
   - I *in seven stages* — 44
   - O *in seven stages* — 46
   - U *in seven stages* — 47

9. The Five Vowels as an Image of Their Nature — 49
   - *The vowels as a process of metamorphosis* — 49
   - *The vowels as an image of the metamorphosis of the I* — 50

10. The Seven Aspects of the I and Their Soul Moods — 52

11. The Whole Human Being in Eurythmy — 55
    - *Eurythmy gestures in anthroposophical terms* — 55
    - *Everyday movement and eurythmy movement* — 56
    - *The dual nature in different parts of the human being* — 56
    - *The whole human being revealed* — 57
    - *Seven steps from sound to speech form* — 58

12. The Seven Modes of the I as Artistic Expression — 60
    - *Seven* Calendar of the Soul *verses as examples* — 60
    - *Five twentieth-century poems as examples* — 64

Part II

13. Zodiac Gestures as Aspects of the Astral Body — 71
    - *From feeling to thinking and from feeling to action* — 72
    - *The inner and outer threshold of the soul* — 73
    - *Three stages of attaining harmony within the soul forces* — 74

14. The Twelve Soul Forms as Artistic Expression — 76
    - *The sources of movement of the three soul forces* — 76
    - *The dynamic sources of other soul forms* — 76

15. The Soul Forms in Walk and Gesture — 79

16. The Soul Forms in Artistic Composition — 81
    - *The* Calendar of the Soul *verses* — 81
    - *Five twentieth-century poems as examples* — 85
    - *A scene from Rudolf Steiner's mystery drama* — 88

17. Rhythmic Alternation Between the Self and the World	90
The soul's breathing between centre and periphery	*90*
The soul's breathing between symmetry and asymmetry	*90*
18. Seven Modes of the I and Twelve Soul Forms	93
19. The Whole Human Being and its Counterimages	96

Part III

20. Planetary Influences and Life Processes	101
21. The Planets Reflected in Human Life	105
The effects of the planets in the seven-year life phases	*105*
Planetary effects and typical attitudes	*106*
Strengths and weaknesses of each planetary type	*107*
The art of living with planetary forces	*109*

Part IV

22. Motifs in Eurythmy Training	113
The first exercises given by Rudolf Steiner	*113*
23. Creative, Formative Processes in Eurythmy	120
The anthroposophical basis for the breathing of the I	*120*
The soul forces as an artistic resource	*121*
The breathing of the I	*121*
Creating forms shaped by the I in the periphery	*122*
Preparing the I for creative activity	*122*
Exercises that reveal the I in the soul	*123*
Exercises that reveal the I in the etheric body	*123*
24. Exercises and Meditations as a Bridge Between the Ego and the I	125
Notes	133
Bibliography	137
Index	139

Translator's note on pronunciation

The vowel sounds in the text follow German pronunciation. Equivalent English approximations are as follows:

A – as in 'ah' (bath)
E – as in 'eh' (bait)
I – as in 'ee' (beet)
O – as in 'oh' (boat)
U – as in 'oo' (boot)
Au – as in 'ow' (bout)
Ei – as in the personal pronoun 'I' (bite)

Preface

From 2000 to 2007, through my work within the Section for Performing Arts, I held many courses and seminars around the world about eurythmy. I felt an increasing obligation to commit the essence of this theme to writing, resulting in this publication. This book, *Planetary Gestures in Eurythmy* is a companion piece to *The Zodiac Gestures in Eurythmy*.

In the first part of this book the seven planetary gestures are described in terms of perspectives of the I and introduced as artistic devices.

The second part is designed to supplement *The Zodiac Gestures in Eurythmy* by depicting the soul forms as gestures of the soul. The seven perspectives of the I combined with the twelve soul forms, will be presented practically as belonging to our store of artistic tools. The eurythmy world in the twenty-first century has the important task of making the whole human being visible. This will consist of listening through and behind speech, heeding and forming the attitude of the I and giving an inner gesture to the connection the soul has to the world by means of eurythmy formation.

The third part will help us get to know how the planetary forces influence us.

The fourth part offers paths of self development, working to bring eurythmy as a bridge from the ego to the I to birth.

I owe a debt of deep gratitude to the scientist Thomas Göbel for his great love of eurythmy. He died in April 2006.

Werner Barfod

Part I

1
Forming the Eurythmy Gestures for the Planets

An overview of the seven gestures

In parallel with the description of the zodiac gestures given in my previous book, *The Zodiac Gestures in Eurythmy,* the gestures for the planets are built up from a colour chord, geometrical shape (straight line or curve) and the movement centre in the human body. The colour triad as an image of the soul comprises a different tone for each element of movement, periphery and form; for instance, Saturn: blue in movement, blue in feeling and blue in character.

Formative forces exist in a bubble-like sphere all around us. Its radius, linking centre and periphery, and setting motion from within, gives rise to the three gestures based on a straight line (Sun, Mercury and Venus). Three other gestures (Mars, Jupiter and Saturn) mark the boundary of the sphere and make its surface wholly or partially visible. The remaining gesture does not share this characteristic, and thus, stripped of movement, appears as a crossing point or midpoint that has come to rest (Moon).

The centre of the gesture changes from form to form, with three having theirs above the heart in the feeling realm (Sun, Mercury, Venus), two originating in the will around the solar plexus (Mars and Jupiter), one coming to rest precisely over this midpoint (Moon), and the final gesture (Saturn) arising from the larynx.

In addition, these gestures need to be produced out of colour on a soul level, out of the finished shape in the etheric and on the basis of three well-defined centre points.

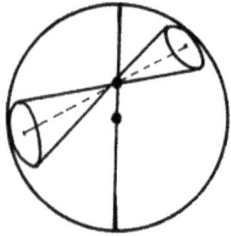
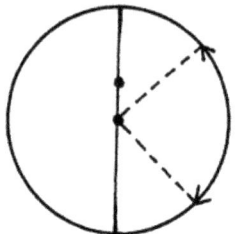

Sun, Mercury, Venus:
Radius moves

Mars, Jupiter, Saturn:
Surface of sphere moves

The seven gestures individually

At the heart of these movements and including them all is the Sun gesture, representing the totality of the human being.

In the speech eurythmy course, *Eurythmy as Visible Speech*, Rudolf Steiner demonstrates the direct possibilities of form and movement that can be developed in human nature, thus introducing a new artistic tool to ally itself microcosmically and macrocosmically to the visible language of sounds.[1]

The *gesture for the Sun,* expressing the *whole human being,* is not only the most perfect, but also encompasses all the others. Its source is the feeling soul realm around the heart, at the height of the breast bone, where the two halves of the collarbone meet. The I sets the outstretched arms in motion here, around an invisible axis, the right one extended upwards and forwards and the left pointing down and back. The human being standing fully within this sphere, touches its inner surface with the fingertips in this rotating gesture.

The gesture's form arises from the colour triad created by the weaving white movement, absorbed by the radial white periphery, that is then drawn towards the centre of the movement formed in white. The upper part of the movement appears symmetrical initially, but gains its ultimate authentic shape when the individual carrying it out is aware of standing on the earth as an upright I-being. The I then senses through the soul how the right half, with the arm stretched up, is directed towards the sense-perceptible visible world, whereas the left arm, pointing downwards, is connected with our slumbering inner forces of will. Our feeling centre holds this shifting equilibrium in check. The innately rhythmical nature of the gesture comes into being out of the dynamic interplay between the I consciously connecting to the outside world through the soul, and taking hold of the sleeping will. The I and soul nature then find full expression in the alternating rhythm of waking and sleeping, experienced as dreamlike movement through the soul that perceives and wills. The individual as a being of I and soul-forces can only be revealed when this gesture appears as alternating dynamic movement.

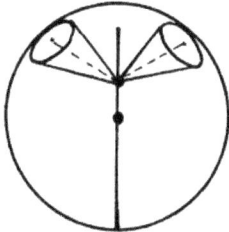 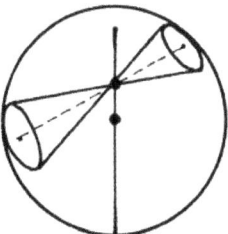

One aspect of the perfection of the Sun gesture is presented in the *loving, selfless human nature* that we see in the *gesture of Venus*. Its source remains the same: the feeling soul. The arms stretch out from the feeling centre in more or less the same position, with the right up and forwards, forming an unmoving, receptive axis, and the left below and behind circling in a mood of surrender. Once more the experience is that of standing in a sphere, touching the inner surface.

The colour triad is created by the balanced green of the movement, the in-breathing and out-streaming green of the periphery, and, finally, the green that is taken in from the outside on the right, coming to rest and then streaming out through the left arm in a mood of devotion. The triad imbues the soul with a sense of surrender to the outside world. The individual seems bound to it in a dreamlike state of self-sacrifice.

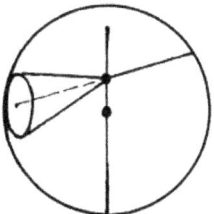

The *self-centred human nature* is revealed in the *gesture of Mercury* that shows the other one-sidedness, the polar opposite to the devotion of Venus. The centre of the movement is the same as before. The extended arms lie on the same axis, with the right arm forwards and up, the left behind pointing down, but here the right arm takes on a dynamic circling motion while the left is called upon to act as a still, unmoving support, thus giving the eurythmist the experience of being the centre of a sphere.

The three aspects of the yellow colour of Mercury manifest as radiant uprightness within the movement, the yellow periphery of the rotation of the right arm, and the left arm raying yellow downwards towards the earth. The gesture has its characteristic shape within the dynamics of the right arm's circling and the left arms's stability. Here the I reveals its place in the soul, asserting itself as central within the physical body.

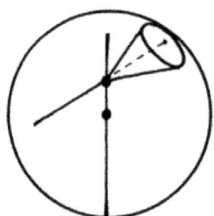

The *Moon gesture* represents an anomaly in so far as it is movement that has come to rest: 'This is in the spiritual realm, so the gesture can remain calm.'[2] Rudolf Steiner places it between the gestures that have been described with their source of movement in our feeling centre, and the remaining three, whose points of origin vary, but which reside ultimately in the region of the will as we shall see. The gesture for *capacity for creation* withdraws fully into the movement centre of the will at the level of the solar plexus, and can be perceived simultaneously as becoming visible, yet apparently at rest. The human being stands in the sphere experiencing the centre in the region of the will, the movement of the gesture comes to a standstill and becomes a position. The gesture initially appears as a picture, with the arms crossed at the wrist, held close to the body. The shoulders, upper arms and forearms together form a pentagon.

The impulse underlying this gesture – the capacity for creation – lies in the way the movement of the Moon flows imperceptibly around the other six planets in the form of a lemniscate. The crossing point is the gesture itself, with the upper loop surrounding the centre of feeling and taking in the gestures of the aforementioned three planets, and the lower loop penetrating far into the periphery, open to the other three gestures that focus on the centre of the will area.

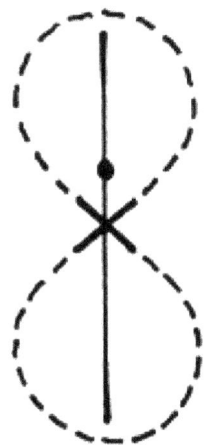

Movement that has come to a standstill – existing in the spiritual world – creating a dreaming rhythmic centre-point within the seven gestures

With the *Mars gesture* – the human *capacity for aggression* – we come to the largest spherical planet gesture. The core of the movement lies within the centre of the will, around the solar plexus. Here a mobile sphere is the source of the gesture, with the arms serving as the radii that set it in motion. The upright human figure, held firm by the feeling centre, is now forced to unite what comes from the periphery with the centre of the will. The arms, held straight, yet with slightly curled fingers, move up and down together with the upper body, while the shoulders are held still. The arm and upper body movement begins at head level, descending to the knees, and rising more loosely back up to the vertical, describing a sphere at body height. This movement places the person carrying it out within the sphere itself.

From the three aspects of red that belong to Mars, the red movement, bracing itself against the earth, rises heavenwards, the red in the periphery pushes against this expression of uprightness, and the formative power of the red character takes hold of the physical body in the will centre as it moves forwards. With the release of these shaping forces, the individual rediscovers the vertical within. Thus the capacity for aggression is experienced as a force that takes hold of the whole body.

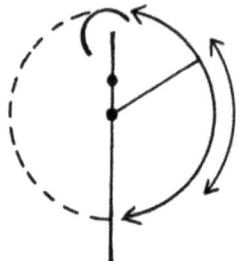

Only part of the sphere is visible – most of it remains invisible

The *gesture of Jupiter*, representing the human *wisdom-imbued activity*, creates the middle sphere. Once again, the origin of the movement is to be found in the centre of the will, but with the entire sphere appearing this time in front of it. This energy is so powerful that the left arm replicates the unmoving source in front of the body, and the right arm completes a spherical streaming movement around it as if flowing from it. The upright human being seems to bestow the power of wisdom from a divinely created reservoir of will forces.

From the threefold nature of the orange ascribed to Jupiter, the movement element breathes out into the world and streams back in to be absorbed. Reinforced by the orange in the periphery, it then becomes wisdom-imbued activity through the forming character of orange.

The *Saturn gesture*, representing *self-containment and deep contemplation*, shows the smallest sphere of movement. It was once the largest in the dawn of evolution, when the human form was a large transparent ball of will. Over time, the ball shrank, hardened and shifted upwards to become the human head, whereas the rest of the human form, connecting with the earth, elongated into trunk and limbs.

The centre of movement for the Saturn gesture is no longer the seat of the will, but the larynx. The gesture starts at the forehead and reaches its lowest point at the diaphragm. Only a small part of the sphere is visible, with the greater part remaining unseen. Our attention is directed inwards and behind, towards the spiritual world.

In the triad of Saturn's dark blue, the movement creates a protection, condensing it out of the blue of the periphery and compressing it so that it compels the hands to assume their position one on top of the other to form the small sphere.

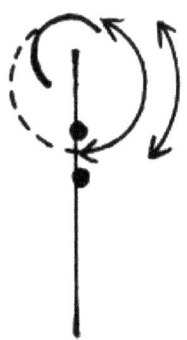

The human being: both centre and sphere in the gestures

In Sun, Venus and Mercury, we experience ourselves as centred in our daytime consciousness. In the Sun gesture that expresses the *complete human being,* the aspect of the soul that is awake and active through the senses, feels its connection to its sleeping will-based counterpart. Through inner work, we can learn how to influence both sides effectively. In the *loving devotional nature* of our soul we meet the needs of the outside world whereas, in contrast, the *self-centred, egotistic nature* of our soul feels itself as the centre of experience.

In Mars, Jupiter and Saturn, we feel ourselves to be like a sphere, set passively in motion from outside as if asleep, yet also placed at the centre of the spherical movement. Mars' *capacity for aggression* is active in our organism through speech and actions; Jupiter's character of *wisdom-imbued activity* arises within the living entity itself, whereas Saturn's *deep contemplation* connects us with our destiny and higher self.

The Moon's *capacity for creation* withdraws and contracts into the centre of the will, renouncing all outer movement and coming to rest. Here, too, the human being lives in the periphery in a dreamlike state, but precisely because of this, has the ability to move, change and create.

At this juncture, it should be clear what Rudolf Steiner meant when he refers to the possibilities for movement that can be discerned in the human organism and ultimately lead back to the sounds of speech.[3] He saw the differentiated faculties and abilities within the microcosmic human, in whom spiritual forces have been active through movement and form prior to birth. He created appropriate gestures enabling the eurythmist to animate the soul through the I and express individual creativity. These artistic elements by which the I finds expression in the soul can be added to the sounds – those elements working on the level of the etheric body. The task of eurythmy in the twenty-first century is to turn these modes of expression into outward form. Chapter 3 presents this in detail including, specifically, the seven modes of being which underlie the artistic activity of the I in the soul that functions in speech.

2

The Characteristics of the Planetary Gestures

The earliest description of the seven gestures is to be found in notebook entries addressed to Erna Wolfram van Deventer in 1914, which have since been published in facsimile with the twelve zodiac gestures in *Eurythmy: Its Birth and Development*. After being described in 1914, the performance indications were taken up and slightly expanded in 1924, in particular with regard to the essential characteristics and sound relationships of the gestures.[1]

Rudolf Steiner refers to the gestures as potential movements of the human organism when considered in its entirety:

> Through human gestures and the possibility of movement, precisely something cosmic is expressed ...
>
> [It is] the imitation of that which was spoken by the gods from heaven down to human beings ... One must only once again discover the potential for really seeking the inner meaning for the corresponding gestures out of the essence of spiritual knowledge ...
>
> Here we proceeded from the human being and went the other way ... from the possibilities of movement and follow the path to the human being, to the visible speech.[2]

Mars: the upper body is rocked up and down with the arms stretched out in front and the fingers drawn inwards. (1914).[3] Addition (1924): with the body, the vowel *E* is given.[4]

Jupiter: the right arm makes a circular movement around the left, which is held in front. Addition (1924): the left arm is also bent inwards and the vowel *O* is given.

Saturn: the hands are turned inwards and placed against the forehead where they are moved smoothly and regularly down and back up. Addition (1924): the hands are placed one over the other on the forehead and the vowel *U* is given.

Sun: the arms are extended with the right up and forwards and the left held down and back, both moving in a circle. Addition (1924): both go round simultaneously and the diphthong *Au* is added.

Venus: the left arm moves in a circle behind while the right is stretched forwards and stays still. Addition (1924): the vowel *A* is given.

Mercury: the right arm makes a circular movement forwards while the left arm stays behind, unmoving. Addition (1924): the contrast to the previous (Venus), and *I* is given.

Moon: The forearms are crossed in front ... As we are here in the spiritual world, they can stay immobile – movement that has come to rest. Addition (1924): accompanied by the diphthong *Ei*.

In the speech eurythmy course in 1924, the most significant addition is the character of the seven gestures: 'we see the human being, as it were, divided into his various capacities, members, and forces.' A little later in the same lecture Rudolf Steiner looks at 'all those qualities that the human being possesses in his activities that stream outwards'.[5]

Here he first described the seven planetary gestures as follows:

Sun: the expression of the whole human being.
Venus: a loving devotional being.
Mercury: an egotistic being.
Moon: the capacity for creation, a creative, productive being
Mars: the capacity for aggression.
Jupiter: the activity or being that arises out of wisdom.
Saturn: contemplation, introspection and self-containment.

3

The Seven Attitudes of the I in the Soul

The dual form of the human members

A threefold principle in the execution of the seven gestures in eurythmy has become evident. On the one hand, the three forces of thinking, feeling and will come through in the shaping of the gestures, and on the other, waking, dreaming and sleeping consciousness are to be found in the threefold formation of the gestures – centripetal (Sun, Mercury and Venus), centrifugal (Mars, Saturn and Jupiter) and the balanced middle (Moon), as in the crossing point of a lemniscate.

The dual nature of each human member underlies this formative principle of the gestures. As the oldest member, the physical body has had from time immemorial a form that is of soul-spirit provenance, as well as an earthly aspect that is filled with matter.

The external aspect of the etheric body, turned towards the outer world, has the faculties of speech and movement, whereas the inner aspect provides the faculties of cognition, imagination and consciously guided processes of the will as instruments to the soul. These dual aspects sum up the achievement of the etheric body. We shall return to this subject in Chapter 5 in relationship to the mysteries of Ephesus.

This twofold principle appears in the soul as form and content. The forms are described by Rudolf Steiner in the lecture of July 7, 1924, in *Eurythmy as Visible Speech,* in terms of the twelve facets of the human soul. The form of the astral body also remains bound up with the physical body when we are asleep. In sleep the soul, permeated by the I, leaves the body. It then, on our waking, fills the form of the astral body and has at its disposal the seven attitudes of the I. These seven gestures will be examined further in terms of their artistic function in eurythmy.

The I also has two states of being: firstly that of the spiritual core, which strives towards its future goal from incarnation to incarnation, and secondly that of our sense of self that constitutes our consciousness. The I both reflects the outer world and experiences itself within it.

Eurythmy has the task of building a bridge that leads from the I in the sense-perceptible world to the objective gestures of the supersensible world that are borne by the periphery.

The seven faculties of the I in the soul

The I as a being of breath is active through every part of the human being. This will be described further in Chapter 4. For the moment, we shall examine the seven ways in which the I manifests in the soul.

In the gesture for the *Sun,* referred to by Rudolf Steiner as the expression of the whole human being, the I exists within the very depths of the soul, the feeling centre for all movement. It mediates in a dreaming state of equilibrium between the wakeful action produced in the upper part and the sleeping movement of the lower one, between sense perception and the impulse of the will. The soul lives within this embracing gesture in a mood of attentive awareness, breathing between centre and periphery.

In the gesture for *Venus,* described as a being of loving devotion, we experience the one-sidedness of the soul that is given over to the outside world and, taking it in, demonstrating the ability to internalise this experience.

In the *Mercury* gesture, the egotistic nature, we acknowledge ourselves at the centre of our surroundings, keen to attract attention and communicate with others.

It should be stressed once more that these soul qualities are seen as a state of being that shows up in the etheric as a multitude of emotions, such as enthusiasm, yearning, devotion, reverence and sorrow, resignation or courage, hope or even fear born from personal experience.

In terms of the characteristic that the I shows in the soul, the three attributes that belong to an awake person stand in contrast to the three that lie in a slumbering will. These gestures are centred around the solar plexus, the focal point of the will. But they are also formed from the periphery, not from the radius, so that the surrounding sphere shapes the gesture.

Practising to acquire a skill, we need to harness and direct the will that works out of the goal of ultimately mastering the ability. Then the movement is guided by that ability into the present. Consciousness steers the will out of the peripheral future into activity. Whereas the I is present and attentive in the periphery, the will intervenes in the opposite direction, centring from the I into the soul.

In the *Mars* gesture, described as the capacity for aggression, the will is turned outwards towards the surroundings. From the periphery, the will intervenes to bend the upright human form around its centre. Then, as if in the moment of respite after this intervention, the upright human form is restored and stands in the centre of the sphere.

Only the wisdom activity of the *Jupiter* gesture shows the entirety of the sphere. It appears on the level of the centre of the will. Here, too, the forces of will in the periphery take hold of the circling form of the movement.

With *Saturn,* described as deep contemplation, the attention of the will is aimed upwards and backwards towards consciousness, thus becoming the drive towards cognition, which opens our own inner spiritual experience.

After these two trios of gestures – the one trio acting centrifugally, the other centripetally – we arrive at the seventh gesture, which holds the balance between inner and outer space at the crossing of the lemniscate. The *Moon* gesture, the potential for creativity, expresses the interplay between will and consciousness.

The birth of any ability derives from the exchange between the waking and the sleeping I. The I is tied into the future of the will and connected with the goal-mastering abilities and skills.

We have presented the contents as creative means of expression. The sphere corresponds to the forms of the astral body. The artistic means described are able to reveal the supersensible aspect of the human being that underlies every speech utterance, showing the bearing of the I.

4
The I as a Being of Breath

The I manifested in twelvefold, sevenfold and threefold form

The I enters the physical body, creating inner and outer dimensions through the twelve senses in their relationship to the soul.

In the time-organism of the etheric body, the I is revealed through the seven life processes both in the natural world and in the cultural realm. We shall return to these in the next chapter.

The I comes to light in a threefold way in the soul in thinking, feeling and will, and can be experienced as self-awareness. Our limbs are asleep, but the I can initiate volitional intention through the body that serves as an instrument of the soul. We dream in the emotional domain, but can also understand through our feelings how to activate the power of judgment.

The I acts as the observer when we consciously perceive.

The rhythm of the I reflected in the members

The I exists as a breathing being in the pulse that links centre and periphery. The smallest rhythm of the I in the body is that of breathing. When speaking, the I is completely focused as if breathing in, whereas it breathes out when it is listening to another with total interest.

The longer rhythm of the I is waking and sleeping: an inhalation into the physical body on awakening and an exhalation into the surroundings when falling asleep.

The greatest rhythm is of birth and death, when the spirit-soul with its life organisation enters the body at birth and leaves it at death, dissipating into the surrounding world of spirit.

The I is active in the soul in a centred and centring way through working on the sleeping will with intentionality, and in a peripheral way in the realm of ideas, of concepts.

The rhythm of the I provides the soul with restraint and structure out of the future. It is able to observe, but not unite with the object. When we practise and perform eurythmy, active powers of judgment are at work, but in a dreaming fashion. In a eurythmy performance, the movement flows out of the tableau created while practising, that is but a shadow of the imagination of the I. This then becomes visible as an artistic product in eurythmy by virtue of the soul's activity.

The archetypal gesture of contraction and expansion

The archetypal human gesture of contraction and expansion can be seen in the four levels of the human being:

- In the *physical body* we can sense the flexing and stretching of the limbs, and indeed the whole human form.
- In the realm of the *etheric* or *life forces,* we breathe in and out, following the course of the sun through day and night, summer and winter, etc.
- On a *soul level,* the gesture is expressed through laughing and crying, in 'lifting of the inner [nature] above the outer [world], so that the inner looks down in laughter ... But when this inner nature feels itself weak towards outer events ... [it is expressed] in crying.'[1]
- On the *level of the I,* which at the same time is that of shaping and forming, the gesture is expressed in simultaneous contraction and expansion. This concurrence also comes to light in form and gesture, in self and the world. All sound gestures as expressions of speech share a common ground between movement (feeling entering from the outside) and character (forming).[2]

5
Planetary Influences in Prenatal and Earthly Existence

Human beings reincarnate. Their cosmic task is to overcome earthly death and their earthly task is to acquire cosmic consciousness.

Rudolf Steiner describes the etheric body as an organism with seven different life processes. We shall try to supplement his description with the seven planetary processes as they influence life before birth and how they support the physical body.

At the age of seven, part of the etheric body becomes free from supporting the development of the physical body and is then available for the soul. The etheric body is inherited and needs to be individualised in stages.

Human abilities as a reflection of prenatal lunar forces

Rudolf Steiner spoke of this enigma at Easter 1924 in connection with the mysteries of Ephesus.[1] The following is based on work done together with Thomas Göbel.[2]

The initiates in Ephesus would be transported back to a pre-birth state, to the sphere of the Moon when the etheric body became more dense. The Moon-beings would weave the exterior of the etheric body from the sunlight reflected by the Full Moon. Mars-beings endowed the etheric body with the gift of speech, whereas their counterparts on Mercury provided the ability to move. Through these faculties of the etheric body, we are able to be active in the world as social human beings.

The spiritual aspect of the New Moon weaves the interior of the etheric body. Out of their experiences in the Jupiter sphere, Moon-beings receive the virtue of wisdom that streams through humans. Love and beauty are bestowed by the Moon-beings to the human soul out of their experiences on Venus, and the warmth of feeling impressed on the etheric body is the result of their exchanges with Saturn.

Jupiter, Venus and Saturn give the etheric body the basis from which it can serve human beings. The I is aided by the etheric in the process of thinking, given by Jupiter's wisdom. The soul is enriched by the etheric that receives imagination from Venus. The warmth forces of Saturn are impressed on the etheric body and are available to the will.

All these properties, emanating from our pre-earthly existence, can be called 'cultural' achievements of the etheric body, in contrast to the natural aspects of the etheric. The exterior of the etheric body holds the potential for language and movement, and forms the basis for learning to speak and walk. The inner aspect of the etheric gives the foundation on which human beings can encounter the world with imagination, develop the power of thinking and establish the potential to work out of the warmth of the will.

Learning to walk and speak precedes the earliest experience of the self in human development. The first experience of the self (marked by saying 'I') is a transition from the outer to the inner side of the 'cultural' etheric body. The latter supports the development of imagination, thinking and everyday skills in actions. All these faculties can be developed further throughout a lifetime of learning.

The natural part of the etheric, the part close to the natural world, needs a healthy natural environment in order to sustain and build up the physical body. It is also a prerequisite for a balanced consciousness. Sleep is the restorer of forces that are eroded during the day.

All human activity has a health-promoting or a detrimental effect on the part of the etheric connected to nature. Human activity is initiated by the I and the soul, which masters the natural side of the etheric body, wresting it from etheric life.

The seven life processes of the natural and 'cultural' etheric

We shall examine the natural processes within the etheric body as well as the way that the I and soul work from the 'cultural' etheric in order to evolve abilities from its inner and outer aspects.[3]

Life processes	'Cultural' processes of the inner side of thinking, imagination and will			'Cultural' processes of the outer side language and movement	
breathing	reading	} enlivening the senses		articulation	} abilities needed to use the physical body
warming	perception/ remembering			sounding	
nutrition	individualisation		all skills for using thinking and imagination	dynamics	
secretion	questioning				
maintaining	interweaving of concepts	} ensouling the life processes			
growth	ideas as tools				
reproduction	meditation				

The etheric body

Rudolf Steiner touched on the subject of eurythmy in connection with the outer aspect of the etheric:

> If people desire to speak in accordance with these Mysteries of the Moon at the present time, it is possible to give expression to them in an entirely different form: this can be done by means of eurythmy. Eurythmy develops out of speech. Having investigated the mysteries of language, by allowing the Moon-beings to instruct us in what they are able to observe when gazing on Mars, we make further investigations. We then notice how what we investigate changes, if, after having directed out observation to Mars, we direct it to Mercury. Thus when we turn from what the Moon-beings experience through Mars to what they experience with regard to Mercury, we pass from the human aptitude for the production of sound to the human aptitude for eurythmy. This is to explain the matter in its cosmic aspect.[4]

The inner and outer aspects of the 'cultural' etheric body both contribute to the acquisition of skills needed for eurythmy. Only once individuals have developed their skills to a dignified level, can specialisation within a particular profession equate to the development of humanity. Guaranteed personal freedom is needed if eurythmy is to be represented independently in the world, assuming that the anthroposophical foundations for it have already been laid.

The planetary forces in Rudolf Steiner's Ephesus verse

Even today, the human etheric body is created by Moon-beings. Rudolf Steiner sums up this process of building up an etheric body, which can foster a culture-promoting capacity in humans, in the following verse:

> Thou Being, offspring of worlds, who in thy light-form
> art strengthened by the Sun under the Moon's control,
>
> Thou art endowed by Mars with his creative resonance,
> with Mercury's swinging movement of thy limbs;
>
> Enlightened by the rays of Jupiter's wisdom,
> and by the love-bearing beauty of Venus,
>
> And Saturn's age-old spiritual inwardness
> consecrates thee to the life in space, to growth in time![5]

The seven modes of being of the I in the soul comprise the totality of potential capabilities latent in the etheric. The illustration below follows the sequence of planets presented in the Ephesus verse.

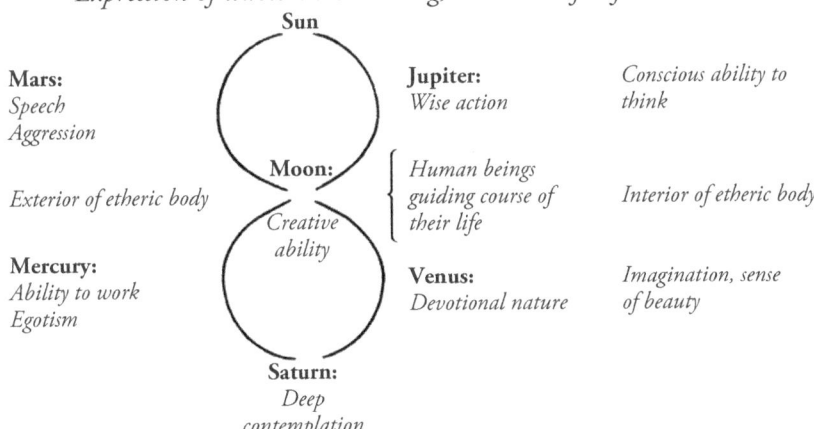

Expression of whole human being, conscious of self

Sun

Mars: *Speech / Aggression*

Exterior of etheric body

Mercury: *Ability to work / Egotism*

Moon: *Creative ability*

Jupiter: *Wise action*

Human beings guiding course of their life

Venus: *Devotional nature*

Conscious ability to think

Interior of etheric body

Imagination, sense of beauty

Saturn: *Deep contemplation*

The artistic human being turned to the spiritual world

The seven life processes as the working of the etheric body

We have highlighted the correspondences between the natural and 'cultural' processes of the etheric body. We have also enumerated a sevenfold sequence of I and soul attributes available for thinking, imagination and volition. Here we shall examine the workings of the etheric body that underlie all forms of practice. These are basic processes that give rise to ways of learning and practising exercises artistically. The first three deal with creating a connection with the material through analysis, the last three have a synthesising character, in the middle between them is an attitude of inquiry.

The natural side	The 'cultural' side
After Rudolf Steiner	*After Christof Lindenau*
Absorbing	Perceiving
Adapting	Noticing, uniting with
Repulsing	Distinguish, differentiate, demarcate
Secretion	Question, showing interest
Preservation	Connecting, making whole
Growth	Become an organ, act out of matter in hand
Production	Renewing, bringing to light again

The basis of the seven life processes

The point of departure is always to ask the right questions and to show interest. Our questions may go in two directions: firstly, to fully comprehend something, or secondly, to look into its context and see the whole picture. The concern of the enquiring individual lies somewhere in the middle and is ultimately all-inclusive. In practice we always move (or even jump) between each group. Experience teaches us to be vigilant, and that a step back can sometimes take us out of an impasse.[6]

Seven steps for practising eurythmy

A tried and tested *first step* in practising eurythmy, involving absorbing and perceiving, is the exercise of contraction and expansion. Eurythmists straight away live with the question of their standpoint in relation to the piece of speech or music to be performed. How do they breathe on a soul level with the speech or music through the gesture? Rudolf Steiner's weekly verses in the *Calendar of the Soul* are a wonderful field to explore, giving eurythmists the chance straight away to find their place from motif to motif in the relationship between soul and the world.

The *second step* is to take note of and to unite with a subject. That means paying close attention and discovering how 'spirit in matter' appears in colours, sounds and images, fostering close observation.

The *third step* is to identify the artistic elements that suit a particular poem or piece of music. In other words, to show how I relate to the world in various settings.

In the *fourth step,* having researched three different levels of practice, we are now ready to ask further questions with a similar approach.

The *fifth step* involves finding our way towards living within the entirety? Do the artistic means we have used correspond to the totality? Now the all-inclusive view that we have of the whole, dictates the evolving form.

The *sixth step* follows. This is to become completely one with what is being fashioned, to become an organ of perception that allows action out of the thing itself.

Thus prepared, the *seventh step* is a matter of bringing the finished form into being out of the etheric tableau itself with complete presence of mind.

6
The Planetary Processes in Varying Sequences

The sequence working in the etheric body

When learning a new skill, we are subject to a sequence of influences from the furthest reaches of the cosmos to the earth itself:[1]

1. Perceive – Saturn process
2. Take note, uniting with – Jupiter process
3. Distinguish, differentiate – Mars process
4. Question – threefold Sun process
5. Connect, make whole – Venus process
6. Become a sense organ – Mercury process
7. Renew, bring into being – Moon process

The path to earth in the Moon sphere

The Ephesus verse lets us experience through Artemis in the Moon sphere how the seven planetary forces lay down and impress potential abilities on the etheric body.

> Thou Being, offspring of worlds, who in thy light-form
> art strengthened by the Sun under the Moon's control,

> Thou art endowed by Mars with his creative resonance,
> with Mercury's swinging movement of thy limbs;

> Enlightened by the rays of Jupiter's wisdom,
> and by the love-bearing beauty of Venus,

And Saturn's age-old spiritual inwardness
consecrates thee to the life in space, to growth in time!

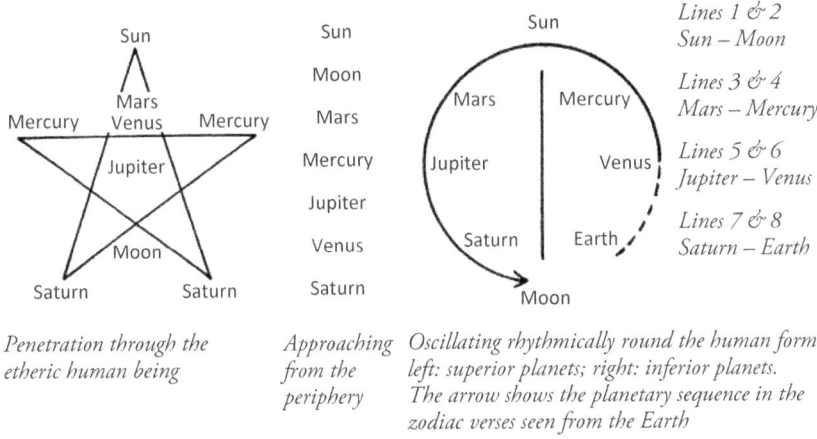

Penetration through the etheric human being   *Approaching from the periphery*   Oscillating rhythmically round the human form left: superior planets; right: inferior planets. The arrow shows the planetary sequence in the zodiac verses seen from the Earth

The goddess Artemis appears in the aura of the Sun, garlanded with the circle of the zodiac, displaying an abundance of fertility forms with figures of animals right down her body, and crescent moons down her back. In the world ether the human soul perceives its own potential being descending towards a new incarnation. Here the shining form of the etheric body in the Moon sphere is experienced.

The planetary sequence in Rudolf Steiner's *Twelve Moods*

In Rudolf Steiner's cosmic poem *Twelve Moods,* each of the twelve verses contains seven lines always in the same order. The Sun begins and, in the seventh line, the Moon reflects it. The soul's spiritual path is mapped out in twelve ways.

As an example we shall take the Aries verse:

Sun	Arise, O shining light,
Venus	Take hold of growth's becoming,
Mercury	Lay hold of the weaving of forces,
Mars	Yourself ray forth, life-awakening.
Jupiter	In face of resistance, gain,
Saturn	In stream of time, disperse.
Moon	O shining light, abide.

1. Development starts with the Sun: the physical foundation becomes denser.
2. Venus grasps what is alive: the etheric foundation becomes denser.
3. Mercury takes hold of the soul: the astral foundation becomes denser.
4. Mars marks the turning point in the I: the Logos being.
5. In Jupiter the foundation for future forces of wisdom belonging to the nature of spirit-self are laid down.
6. With Saturn the divine power of memory belonging to our life-spirit nature is established.
7. The Moon manifests the chalice that contains the sunlight of spirit man.

When the *Twelve Moods* are performed in eurythmy, the stage arrangement devised by Rudolf Steiner shows all the planets aligned on a radius of the zodiac linking the heliocentric with the geocentric planetary order. The Moon represents the Earth in the centre. There then follow the inner planets, Mercury and Venus. At the centre of the planetary line, the Sun moves twenty-four times through the entire circle during the twelve verses and the transition to each verse. The outer planets, Mars, Jupiter and Saturn, are on the outside of the line, towards the zodiac.

Rudolf Steiner was able to conceive the planetary and zodiac dances afresh with this arrangement on stage.

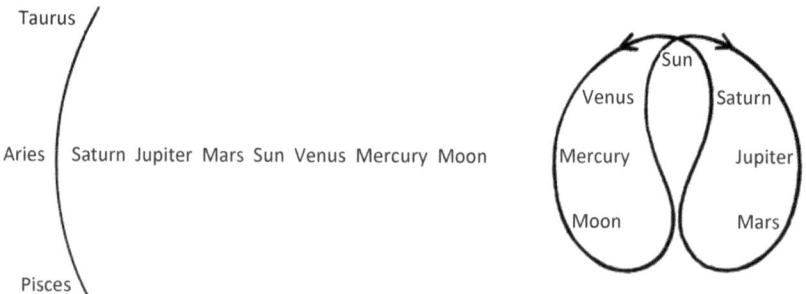

Planetary circle with the wings of the harmonious lemniscate showing inner and outer planets respectively

The planetary sequence in evolution

In the sculpted forms on the capitals of the two sets of seven columns supporting the great dome of the first Goetheanum, the planets appear as images of earthly and human evolution. The metamorphosis of the forms, manifesting planetary processes, took place between an upper open periphery and a lower contracted centre.

Rudolf Steiner provided inscriptions for each column that accompanied the progression from our divine surroundings to the human I and finally to the union of the divine with humanity.[2]

Saturn capital: THE IT	Primordial state of warmth, human beings are spherical beings. Nowadays: *contemplation.* In music: prime interval.
Sun capital: TO IT	The human space relating to love, light and life. Nowadays: the *expression of the whole human being.* In music: second.
Moon capital: IN IT	The concept of the human bodily form. Nowadays: the *capacity for creation.* In music: third.
Mars capital: I	The power of speech. The mystery of Golgotha. Nowadays: the *capacity for aggression.* In music: fourth.
Mercury capital: FROM THE I	The power of movement. Nowadays: *egotistical nature.* In music: fifth.
Jupiter capital: OUT OF ME	The entire organism is fulfilled. Nowadays: *wisdom-imbued activity.* In music: sixth.
Venus capital: I INTO IT	The future I-soul. Nowadays: *loving, devotional nature.* In music: seventh.

7
The Seven Vowel Responses of the Etheric Body

The seven ways in which the I lives in the soul impress their eurythmy gestures on the etheric body. They are visible as six moving gestures and one that has come to rest, arising in this form from the very origins of eurythmy movement in the feeling and willing soul. The etheric body serves the I and soul by enabling the shaping of form. As a reaction to this imprinting, the etheric body responds like an echo with the corresponding completion of the gesture of the vowel. The feeling centre of the soul is the responsive source of all vowels. The vowel gesture arises like an after-image when the planetary movement is released, comes to rest, and allows the etheric body to generate its counterpart. Just as these planetary gestures are at home in the soul, so do the vowels live in the etheric. This is naturally a subtle process, akin to meditation, that can only be hinted at. Reflecting the way in which the seven modes of being were described in Chapter 1, their equivalent vowels will be shown here.

The *Sun gesture* – as expression of the entire human being – touches the movement-sphere from within, making a circling motion with the right hand above and with the left below. The raying-out activity and its complementary accompaniment alternate in energy upwards to the front and downwards behind, giving the Sun gesture its dynamics.

By means of this changing character of left and right, of streaming out and taking in, the etheric response has no choice but to be twofold. According to the side on which the intensively radiating-out energy is sustained, its etheric response is an in-streaming motion. Correspondingly, if one side has an energy that is receptive and flowing in, the gesture on the other side responds by raying out. Since these tendencies need to align and connect left and right, an outstretched in-streaming position is assumed with one arm, forming a half an *A*, and an out-streaming gesture with the other, forming half an *U*. In this way the diphthong *Au* arises, displaying the dual activity of in-streaming and out-streaming.

The *Venus gesture* – loving devotion – demonstrates the one aspect of the Sun gesture, complete devotion, as it takes in its surroundings on the right side and will-imbued devotion on the left. With Venus, however, the right side has become a resting radial line, while there is a wilful outpouring activity through the left.

The etheric body responds within the resonance of this gesture with its own movement that both flows in to and absorbs from the surroundings, by adding to it with the appearance of *A*.

The *Mercury gesture* – the egotistical nature – demonstrates the other extreme to be found in the Sun gesture. The extended, dynamic right arm emphasises the strong impulse to come to oneself in terms of taking hold of the movement at its source in the soul. The unmoving left side is pulled down towards the earth and is felt to provide a solid support. The etheric response to the planet gesture is to seize the source of the movement in the soul and to send it raying upwards through the right arm, while maintaining stability through the downward pointing left arm with the vowel *I*.

The exception amongst these modes of being is the *Moon gesture*, depicting movement that has settled into stillness. Its crossing point, held against the body, becomes an image pointing to the centre of the will. Taking a place between the three upper and three lower gestures, it acts as their mirror, absorbing their movements through the will and transforming them into the capacity for creation. The response in the etheric is a vowel gesture that glides out of an *E* crossing to the lemniscate formed by the in- and out-streaming in the surrounding space of *I*, giving rise to the diphthong *Ei*.

The capacity for aggression expressed by the *Mars gesture* has its main source in the will. The gesture is defined by the sphere of which it is part, depriving the eurythmist of verticality in the rhythmic swinging movement, but giving back an even stronger expression of will. The gesture for Mars brings us to that other planetary trinity that generates sphere-shaped activity within, but on an unconscious level. The unpleasant sensation of being constantly torn out of an upright posture through the rounding of the body is registered by the etheric. The antidote to this force is to awaken the will by means of the *E* crossing.

The wisdom-imbued activity of the *Jupiter gesture* points to the centre of its own complete sphere made just in front of the seat of the will. The self-contained integrity of centre and circumference gives rise to controlled stillness. The etheric reaction to this state of active tranquillity is to produce a form that is both bound up with the outside world and also encloses a portion of it – the *O*.

The *Saturn gesture,* denoting contemplation, is also something of an anomaly in that the will and movement source are pushed up towards the larynx. The gesture reveals the smallest of all the spheres, with only part of it visible, as it is mostly hidden within the invisible spiritual space behind. The resulting isolation from the anterior soul space is counterbalanced by the etheric body producing a freely flowing assertive *U,* opening up the space behind to feeling and light, breaking through the sense of seclusion.

In this way we can see that the vowels, as a means of artistic expression, are an activity of the etheric body. They have been presented here in contrast to the aforementioned modes, which are instruments of the I channelled through the soul, and, ultimately made visible in the gesture performed by the etheric body.

8
The Seven Levels of Manifestation of the Vowels

Rudolf Steiner said about the vowel sounds, 'When we allow the five vowel sounds to work upon us, we receive the impression of man in his primeval strength and vigour. Man, as it were, is born again in his true dignity.'[1] Human evolution is echoed in the soul by the vowels. Created from the cosmos in *A,* taking hold of the self in *E,* the human being reaches a consciousness of personal individuality in *I.* This generates the inner strength to connect with the world in *O* and to strive to return to the spiritual realm in *U.*

Each vowel appears in many different guises on the levels of body, soul and spirit, with gods and humans active to various degrees in all three. The sounding vowel finds its natural home in the soul – expressing a spontaneous burst of feeling, an inner experience or a response to the outside world. The vowel always remains an expression of the human soul and spirit, touching the world through feeling. By contrast, the consonant condenses itself until it becomes part of the sense-perceptible processes and the expression linking the inner realm of pure being and the workaday world.

Rudolf Steiner gave us the characteristics that apply to the formation, experience and efficacy of the sounds in eurythmy. If we examine them more closely, we uncover a sequence of seven stages, corresponding in the vowel only to the stages of the soul incarnating in the body, than freeing itself again:

1. The cosmic essence of the vowel sound works in creating form.
2. The shaping of the sound becomes a human gesture.
3. The sound turns it into speech in inner experience.

4. The sound experienced as a colour triad.
5. The sound expressing the relationship to the world.
6. The sound in its effect on movement.
7. The human being connects to the cosmos through the sound.

In the following section, these seven levels of the vowels will be outlined with some selected characteristics.[2]

A in seven stages

1. The cosmic essence of the vowel sound works in creating form
'We only understand ourselves as people with true human dignity, when we begin to realise that the gods are radiating their forces into us from the surrounding cosmos.'[3]

It is as if a spiritual element penetrates us that is akin to our soul component and actually splits us in two.

It is the first germ of humankind with the oldest sound (Old Saturn). At that time it was just warmth in and around human beings.

Humanity was in a state of wonder at its very existence – pure amazement.

2. The shaping of the sound becomes a human gesture
'The *A*-experience in the gesture demands a conscious stretching of the muscles. You have to lay hold of the stretched muscles ... With the *A*, we stream centripetally from two different directions into the centre ... [we need] the feeling of laying hold of something ... taking hold of something which comes to meet you.'[4]

3. The sound turns it into speech in inner experience
'The meaning of Alpha ... "The one who experiences his own breathing".'[5]

'When we utter the sound *A* we feel ... that this sound really proceeds from our inmost being when we are in a state of wonder and amazement.'[6]

'When you speak the sound *A*, or fashion it in eurythmy, you cause your astral body to sink down as much as it can into your physical body. This entails a feeling of well-being.'[7]

4. The sound experienced as a colour triad
The *A* comes to life by means of a colour combination: the movement is reddish-lilac, the feeling is greenish-bluish, and the character is light red.

5. The sound expressing the relationship to the world
'And this mood of wonder is felt by the astral body (contained as it is within the physical body, within the whole human being). This mood of wonder must be felt in practising, once or even repeatedly, if the *A* is to be true.'[8]

6. The sound in its effect on movement
'The minor mood is always a retreat into yourself with the soul and spirit part of your being: it is a laying hold of the bodily by the soul and spirit.'[9]

'The *A* counteracts the animal nature in man.'[10]

Our connection to the divine gives us this sound that counteracts the animal nature. The symmetry of the two directions becomes thereby the basis for freedom.

7. The human being connects to the cosmos through the sound
The planetary energy of Venus belongs to *A* – a quality of love and devotion.

'All that permeates our souls as *love* and *beauty*, we receive through the experiences that come ... from Venus.'[11]

E in seven stages

1. The cosmic essence of the vowel sound works in creating form
'When human beings speak the sound *E*, they feel that something spiritual is happening within them.'[12]

This spiritual element seems to enter our own physical body and permeate us.

2. The shaping of the sound becomes a human gesture
'Something has been done to us and we stand firm against it. *E* will not allow what has been done to trouble us.'[13]

Something like a crossing of two streams as an imagination, like the air that is exhaled when *E* is produced.

'The *E*-experience carries with it the necessity that you are aware of resting one arm upon the other, and here your experience is mainly centred at the point of the crossing.'[14]

3. The sound turns it into speech in inner experience
Learn to feel an *E* in every crossing, even if only hinted at, combined with a sense of astonishment.

Also feel every possible nuance of astonishment in the soul – reverence, fear, disgust, etc.

4. The sound experienced as a colour triad
The colours giving the *E* its character are: green in movement, light yellow in feeling and very pale red in the character.

5. The sound expressing the relationship to the world
'We offer some resistance; we confront the world ... We touch ourselves. We say as we experience the *E* sound, "I too am here confronting the world".'[15]

6. The sound in its effect on movement
'The *E* fixes the ego [the I] in the etheric body, it strongly penetrates the etheric body with the ego.'[16]

'Here we have a strong influence which proceeds from the human etheric acting on the astral nature, and which has the effect of warming the circulation.'[17]

7. The human being connects to the cosmos through the sound
Mars belongs to the vowel *E*; it is the force of the capacity for aggression.

We owe the impulse for speech, the faculty of language to this cosmic connection.

I in seven stages

1. The cosmic essence of the vowel sound works in creating form
The *I* is 'an expression for the human being as a person. The entire individual person is thereby expressed.'[18]

When we utter *I*, our spiritual aspect is fixed in us and to some extent filled out by whatever we take into consideration when we look at ourselves.

2. The shaping of the sound becomes a human gesture
I is every form of stretching wherever it is felt – in the arms, legs, in the whole body; but also with the eyes, nose, tongue, even a finger or, if you are able, a toe. The main point is the experience of stretching.

'With the *I* we stream from our centre outwards ... we feel a stretching. We feel that the stream has its source in us, starting as it were from the heart and flowing through the arm.'[19]

3. The sound turns it into speech in inner experience
The individual 'wants to express self-assertion, placing himself in the world.'[20]

'There is a flashing of fire ... you always have the radiating element ... *I* is the true Dionysos.'[21]

'The *I*-sound ... [is] "having been curious about something" and then having understood it.'[22]

4. The sound experienced as a colour triad
Using the tools of colour, the *I* is built up out of yellow-orange in the movement, light red in the feeling and a muted blue in the character.

5. The sound expressing the relationship to the world
I is the sound that comes closest to human nature and identifies itself with a person as an individuality. It is at the same time the centre of experience and the placing of that centre into the outside world.

6. The sound in its effect on movement
'The *I* reveals man as a person.'[23]

'Human beings place their own being into space themselves.'[24]

7. The human being connects to the cosmos through the sound
Mercury belongs to the *I*-sound. It is the planetary energy of the egotistic being.[25]

The breathing movement belongs to the inner movement of the *I*-sound.[26]

O in seven stages

1. The cosmic essence of the vowel sound works in creating form
'When speaking the *O*-sound, human beings should have the sense that the spiritual world is manifested to them.'[27]

When we pronounce the *O*-sound, we are facing a spiritual presence able to declare that something is speaking to us through it.

'In the vowel sound *O*, you have a distinct going-out of the soul from the body.'[28]

2. The shaping of the sound becomes a human gesture
'*O*: every rounding and coming together of the limbs in connection with the feeling of a loving embrace.'[29]

'Make the gesture for *O* in such a way that, from the beginning to end, the arms are really rounded, completely supple, rounded arms from the beginning.'[30]

3. The sound turns it into speech in inner experience
Loving embrace is tied up with a sense of wonder.

'The essential gesture of *O* can be shown when the human being feels not only himself, but reaches beyond to feel something else, or another being, whom he wants to embrace.'[31]

4. The sound experienced as a colour triad
The *O* is reddish in movement, greenish yellow in feeling and blue in character. The mood of *O* needs light colours.

5. The sound expressing the relationship to the world
'In the *O*-gesture the world experiences something through man himself, for in this movement he lays hold of something belonging to the world.'[32]

'With *O* there is a kind of falling-asleep-while-staying-awake, in that you allow your whole being to go for a little walk into the space which you enclose with the *O*-gesture.'[33]

6. The sound in its effect on movement
'The *O* reveals man as soul.'[34]

In the *O*, we leave ourselves but also enclose something inside. The connection is outside but I remain within myself.

7. The human being connects to the cosmos through the sound

The *O* belongs to the planetary force of Jupiter which comprises 'the activity of efficacious wisdom.'[35]

'What is found in human beings as soul qualities ... inclinations, sympathy.'[36]

U in seven stages

1. The cosmic essence of the vowel sound works in creating form

In the *U*-sound, the human soul comes into contact with things that have to do with otherworldly events outside itself and not involving it.

It is like an external spiritual phenomenon, that does not affect the human being directly, but rather demands to be entered into.

2. The shaping of the sound becomes a human gesture

'Every turning upwards ... for example joy, jubilation: "hooray" with a jump or a little skip.'[37]

'I run along my arms when I make the movement for *U*. I am convinced of it, that in *U* I stream away, away, away – away in this direction.'[38]

'*U* is most clearly expressed by holding the arms as near together as possible, but this can also only be indicated. There need only be an indication of this drawing together of the arms. When we stand with our legs together, we are also expressing the sound *U*.'[39]

3. The sound turns it into speech in inner experience

'*U* can be felt as something which inwardly chills the soul, chills, stiffens and rigidifies ... [it] gives us the feeling of coldness. *U*, then, is the chilling, stiffening process.'[40]

You can have the subtle sense that the *U*-sound is expressed in the soul when it is confronted with something eerie, something indistinct and invisible.

4. The sound experienced as a colour triad

The *U*-sound is built up of blue in movement, yellow in feeling and purple in character.

5. The sound expressing the relationship to the world
'The feeling of *U* is that of being bound up with something, yet wishing to get away from it, following the movement you make and going somewhere else, leaving yourself and preparing your way.'[41]

'And when I say that with the sound ... *U* I am going with the astral body out of my physical body, I am speaking in terms of speech.'[42]

6. The sound in its effect on movement
'The *U* reveals man as man [*or*, in our humanity].'[43]

'With the *U* ... the ability to stand firm is called forth.'[44]

An unfamiliar spiritual element that I need to grasp and assimilate, in the hope that it will divulge its secret.

7. The human being connects to the cosmos through the sound
The planetary force of Saturn belongs to *U*.

'A profound inwardness – Saturn.'[45]

'Man is only able to lift himself upright through ... Saturn.'[46]

Saturn imparts 'to the human etheric bodies their inner warmth of soul.'[47]

9

The Five Vowels as an Image of Their Nature

The vowels as a process of metamorphosis

The five vowels taken together form the expression of the human I in the soul. In eurythmy they are all rooted where feeling arises in the soul, yet their source of articulation move from far back in the oral cavity to the front, on the lips. The wellspring for the vowels leaves its first place of contact in the *A,* between the shoulder blades, shifts inwards in *E,* arrives with *I* in the middle of the rib cage, in *O* emerges as a new source outwards to settle at the breastbone, and finally seems to stream through the individual from top to bottom in *U,* which at its narrowest is the width of the spinal column, and at its widest as the shoulders.

A process of metamorphosis takes place here, which seems to stream out of the cosmos towards us in *A* and then released back into spiritual realms in *U.*

We are already familiar with examples of metamorphosis in elements of eurythmy, such as the intervals in music, the exercise 'I think speech' or the evolutionary sequence. The factor that links them is something all-encompassing and loftier that allows the next stage to be revealed. We need to call upon our inner activity in order to relinquish what has just been attained without losing it, and to internalise its essence in order to manifest it once more on a subsequent level.

The vowels as an image of the metamorphosis of the I

If we trace the development of the vowels as Rudolf Steiner characterises them by their spiritual effect on human beings, a clear image of the nature of their metamorphosis emerges.

When we speak *A* it is if a spiritual element penetrates us that is akin to our soul component and actually splits us in two.

A spiritual energy comes towards us from the periphery of the universe, radiating into us from two stellar places, and touching us at a point between the shoulder blades, This spiritual energy is akin to us and renders us open to its influence.

The awareness that something in our surroundings takes notice of us, creates a sense of wonder and astonishment. The experience of this contact becomes internalised, prompting the spiritual world to create the next vowel form, in which the soul, stirred out of sleep by the touch from outside, develops the capacity to construct a crossing.

When we speak *E* the spiritual element seems to enter our own physical body and permeate us. 'When a human being speaks the sound *E*, he feels that something spiritual is happening within him.'[1]

The experience of the *E*, arising from this position of the crossed arms, consists of slight pain –the first awakening into *E*. From there, the process of metamorphosis continues as we move from the awareness of the crossing formed in front of us to an inner confirmation of ourselves as the centre and thus midpoint in a further experience – namely, the capacity to raise ourselves up into the vertical, poised between light and darkness.

When we utter an *I,* our spiritual aspect is fixed in us and to some extent filled out by whatever we take into consideration when we look at ourselves.

Out of our experience of our very centre and of our place in space, the *I*-sound radiates out. Interest in the world around develops from this out-streaming radiance, generating the ability to feel connected to our surroundings.

'When speaking the *O*-sound, human beings should have the sense that the spiritual world is manifested to them.'[2]

In the *O*-sound the human soul is linked to the world in such a way that it surrenders a bit of itself by slipping into something external. From this experience, the ability to expand ever further into the periphery and to engage with it, develops so that it stretches into infinity, with the I and soul freed from the body.

When we speak *U* it is like an external spiritual phenomenon, that does not affect the human being directly, but rather demands to be entered into.

'In the vowel sound *O* or *U*, you have a distinct going-out of the soul from the body ... the astral body and ego leave the etheric and physical bodies, even if this occurs partially and imperceptibly. It is really a falling-asleep-while-still-awake.'[3]

Here we reach the closing of the circle that begins in the realm of the stars with *A*, reaches the central experience of the self in *I* and then takes in the cosmos and extends into infinity with *U*. Our own I is the spiritual component that gradually binds itself to us during our life on earth. Eternal being is drawn in figuratively through the breath during our incarnation on earth to become our everyday self, and is then released into the spiritual world once more. There is only one vowel-being: the I, our innermost self. Through our incarnation, our higher I creates these five vocalic stages as an image of how we experience the self in relation to body and soul during our life. Thus the journey through the vowels as they unfold and reveal themselves is like a picture of the human biography.

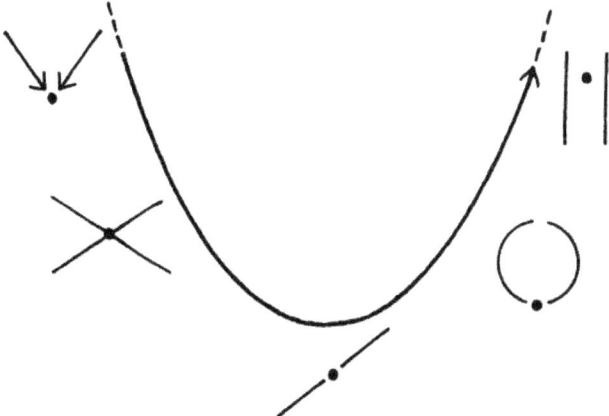

10

The Seven Aspects of the I and Their Soul Moods

Once we have understood that the vowels are an etheric response to the forming of the seven aspects of the I, as described in Chapter 7, we can then turn to the question of the corresponding moods that surface within our soul.

Let us start with the 'expression of the whole human being' that has *Au* as its response. This sound encompasses the inner activity of absorption and radiating in the soul space. A mood of devotion is produced when our source of movement grasps this simultaneous activity. Since the dawn of time, the syllable AUM has exemplified how our breathing soul realm mediates between and connects both the inner and outer worlds. The eurythmy gesture that depicts devotion consists of the upper arms held close to the body, the forearms bent towards the heart and the hands hovering somewhere between *A* and *U*. Rudolf Steiner sets out the various soul moods, referring to devotion as an intensification of knowledge and solemnity.[1] Knowledge is expressed in the bearing with emphasis on the right-hand side, and solemnity stresses the left-hand side and a more passive attitude.

The 'egotistical nature' and the 'capacity for loving devotion' are part of the same formative force that involves the feeling centre and the two radii to the spherical periphery. The *I*-sound lends emphasis to the centre, emerging as self awareness and the voice of conscience in terms of soul mood. In *A*, we open ourselves up to the surrounding world in an attitude of marvelling and wonder.

Thus we have *Au*	devotion – solemnity – knowledge
On one side *I*	self-awareness – voice of conscience
On the other side *A*	marvelling and wonder

10. THE SEVEN ASPECTS OF THE I AND THEIR SOUL MOODS

This is the awake, conscious aspect of the soul moods. On the other side we have aspects tied to the will in the spherical gestures. Here empathy, generosity and sacrifice arise out of the will-bound self or I that is connected to the world. The *O* takes hold of the entire sphere of wise activity generated by the will. The capacity for aggression, characteristic of *E,* reveals the mood that seeks to preserve and transform the self; whereas contemplation is directed towards the innermost depths of the soul.

We now come to darkness as an inner state that evokes fear. This can intensify into despair, yet on the other hand, courage can be summoned – all shades of feeling that belong to *U*.

Thus we have *O*   empathy – generosity – sacrifice
On one side *E*   self-preservation and self-transformation
On the other side *U*   fear – despair – courage[2]

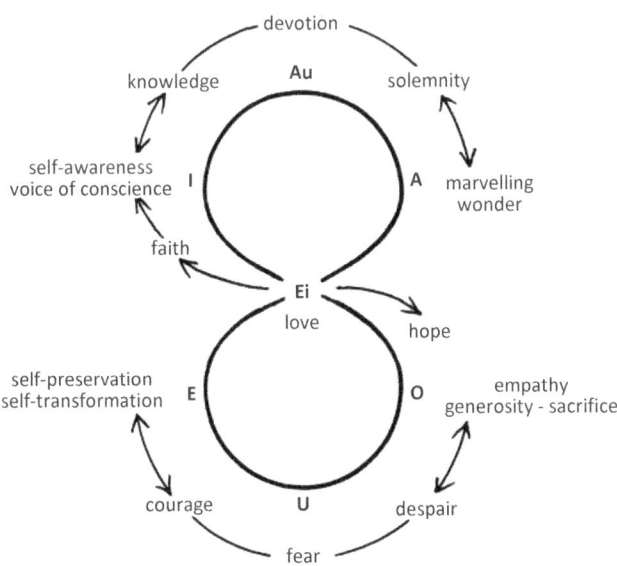

The central gesture of the 'capacity for creation' mediates between the three gestures formed out of the centre and the three out of the periphery. This capacity connects consciousness with the engagement of the will in constant creativity with the sound *Ei*. These two aspects unite freely in the soul as love of duty. When love turns towards knowledge, faith arises; when love turns towards despair, hope provides salvation.

Thus the soul modes of faith, hope and love stand between knowledge and the will in the *Ei*.

The full range of artistic resource in eurythmy has now been described. This brings the whole supersensible human being to life within, through and behind speech. Eurythmy is an art form that makes us so completely visible as to become spiritual.

11

The Whole Human Being in Eurythmy

We shall now demonstrate firstly, the level (in anthroposophical terms) on which a eurythmy gesture appears and where in the body it resides; secondly, how the whole individual, including the four members and their transformation into higher members, manifests; and thirdly, to highlight how the artistic resources correspond to the four members of the whole human being.

Eurythmy gestures in anthroposophical terms

Rudolf Steiner gives various depictions of the level of eurythmy gestures or movement. In a faculty meeting of the eurythmy training in Stuttgart, Rudolf Steiner said with regard to anthroposophy:

> When talking about the physical body, [it can be shown] that through eurythmy to a great extent the movements of the etheric body actually appear instead of the physical body, so that the laws of the physical cease, and the etheric body affects the physical world directly on the physical plane. It works otherwise behind the physical plane. However, that is not all. Here we can show that the physical body steps into the background, is only carried along; the etheric moves in such a way that it is in the physical world. The astral body becomes what the etheric body is otherwise, going over into the I-organisation, so that we have the human being standing already in a higher world. If the physical body is carried up

with it, then it goes beyond the physical laws. When the human being moves in the super-human sphere, the laws of the physical world are no longer the standard.[1]

Everyday movement and eurythmy movement

This process that has been illustrated by Rudolf Steiner can be exemplified in different ways. We plan here to look at everyday intentional movements that are directed towards an object, where the astral body and I are already at the location while the etheric body follows in their wake as the action is executed. A movement in eurythmy is without reference to any external object, but is focused instead on the process of the movement, perceiving the stretching and flexing of the muscles, adding soul-content and giving form through the I. This can be understood if we consider how we can trace the impression of a consonant in everyday movement back to etheric movement, where it is filled with soul-substance.

Chapter 4 illustrated the way in which the I, as a breathing entity, manifests a duality, either turned in towards the centre or out to the periphery. We shall now examine the dual nature of the other members of the human being.

The dual nature in different parts of the human being

In this context, the *etheric body* executes the speech process as a peripheral system. The soul works through the *will* when we breath out, using the muscles of the abdomen. *Feeling* allows the created stream of air to flow through the larynx, sounding a vowel. *Thinking* differentiates the stream in the pharynx and mouth into consonants. The vowels sound inwardly relating to the soul, while the consonants are directed to the outer world. Here, through speech, we can see the processes at work in the etheric body. When vowels and consonants appear in movement in eurythmy, speech becomes visible as a supersensible power of the etheric permeated by the sentient soul.

The *astral body* also has two visible forms that can be used artistically in eurythmy. When our soul turns towards our social environment, we experience shades of feeling that are interwoven with aspects of the sentient and intellectual soul. On the other hand, the astral body can undergo twelve metamorphoses reflecting how the sentient body relates to the world. These remain semi-conscious. Rudolf Steiner refers to these as the twelve zodiac gestures,[2] and they are described in detail, together with another aspect of the consciousness soul, in my book, *The Zodiac Gestures in Eurythmy*.

As an artistic mode of expression these gestures belong to the consciousness soul. Their dual nature is also evident in the six speech gestures, either turning out towards the world or facing in towards the self, in their relationship to the zodiac.[3]

The *I* appears as seven modes of being in the soul, and also appears in the seven corresponding gestures. The source of movement of these gestures varies according to the soul impulse.

All members of the human being reveal the relevant artistic gestures as aspects of the supersensible individual.

The whole human being revealed

The content of speech originates in poetry. Speech sounds out of the I working with different aspects of the soul. The astral body determines the speech gestures that are set to fill it. At the same time, inner attitudes towards the world resonate in the soul. Finally, through the articulated sounds, the etheric body reveals how the human being becomes a Logos-being in the activity of speech. The I works on these members transforming them into seeds of higher members: working from the periphery inwards assumes something of the character of *spirit self,* allowing speech to arise in one of the attributes of the I expresses the seed of *life spirit*.

These gestures that disclose the attitude of the I, are the most transparent and comprehensive to define and sum up the soul forms. These contain both the speech gesture and the mood that surround a motif or a sentence. The sounds enter this forming stream.

New tasks have to be fulfilled if all of this is to be created in an artistic way. Firstly, we need to train our inner ear to listen behind and through speech in order to sense the corresponding attitude towards the world. The resulting possible implementation also needs to be differentiated – whether in solo or group performances – so that the whole human being can appear in the finished structure. This approach allows new possible configurations.[4]

Seven steps from sound to speech form

We have now described the full scope of artistic resources available to the supersensible human being. It may encourage us to become more familiar with them if we set out the seven levels in reverse order, expanding from the individual to the totality, starting with the practice exercises.

1. The metamorphosis from the work-based movements (as in traditional manual work) to consonantal gestures needs no explanation. Eurythmy retains elements of this level in the spatial orientations of heaven and earth, east and west, air and water, etc.
2 and 3. Consonants and vowels are part of speech, showing a person's connection both to the surroundings and to the self in body and soul. They produce syllables and words.
4. With soul dispositions, attitudes and colour moods we arrive at the level on which the I is revealed in the sentient soul. These shades of feeling can embrace a sound, a word, a motif or a sentence. They appear before, during or after a motif as a way of creating form.
5. The six speech gestures colour soul mood in speech. They take effect in the context of a sentence, a line of a poem, a presentation of a thought or image.
6. The twelve ways in which the astral body is revealed show our relationships in a social context. They too can determine a motif, a line of a poem or sentence. Rudolf Steiner's encouragement is to listen behind speech, or to intuit connections with soul and I so that gestures lying within speech are discovered naturally.
7. The modes of being of the I become visible through the eurythmist's own approach. How does the language style challenge me in my feeling, will or thinking? What sort of attitude makes speech visible in a given situation?

11. THE WHOLE HUMAN BEING IN EURYTHMY

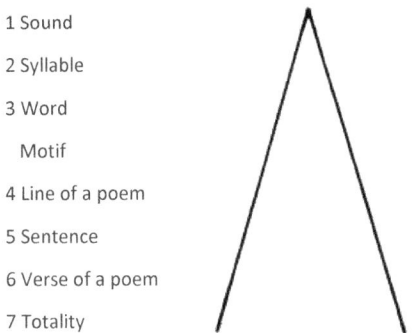

1 Sound
2 Syllable
3 Word
  Motif
4 Line of a poem
5 Sentence
6 Verse of a poem
7 Totality

From single building blocks to totality

The work of the I in the other supersensible members, particularly in the etheric, provides the basis for this process, as described earlier in Chapter 5. I need to find my own vantage point within language – experiencing the specific relationship between self and the breath through expansion and contraction – so that I can establish my own connection to speech and how to form it. A practice of attentiveness can become the path to artistic creation. The mode the I adopts has a determining and overarching function for everything else, be it verse, a prose passage or a character in a play.

A certain amount of preparatory work is needed to integrate the soul form and the mode of the I into an artistic creation without actually showing a gesture. For the modes of the I, the soul aspects of thinking, feeling and willing as a basis in the forming of sounds have already been mentioned.

There are dynamic points of departure in order to create a soul form, which will be described in detail in Chapter 14. It is always a matter of working out of and with the periphery of the I, and simultaneously out of the colour moods and these gestures. This will be followed by a practical demonstration of the seven modes of the I, with the help of selected texts, showing possible ways of producing forms.

12

The Seven Modes of the I as Artistic Expression

Seven *Calendar of the Soul* verses as examples

The 52 weekly verses composed by Rudolf Steiner as the *Calendar of the Soul,* provide a wonderful field for practice. The I learns to breathe rhythmically in these verses: 'A healthy feeling of "at one-ness" with the course of nature, and from this a vigorous "finding of oneself" is here intended.'[1]

At first it is simply a question of inwardly accompanying every breath of the I in the verses, as it swings back and forth between inner and outer world, contraction and expansion, all the while aware of its own perspective, and sensing which of the seven modes speaks at any given time. Seven verses have been selected as examples.

Week 1
Beginning of April – Easter mood

When out of world-wide spaces
The sun speaks to the human mind,
And gladness from the depths of soul
Becomes, in seeing, one with light,
Then rising from the sheath of self,
Thoughts soar to distances of space
And dimly bind
The human being to the spirit's life.

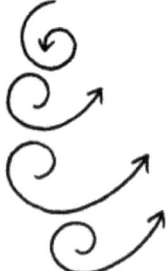

The *Sun as expression of the whole human being,* lives in this verse. Its light aspect breathes at the beginning, followed by the duller side, which reaches out into cosmos. As eurythmists we stand firm within the feeling centre of the movement.

A subsequent task when giving the verse aesthetic shape would be to divide it into four parts.

Week 11
Third week in June

> In this the sun's high hour it rests
> With you to understand these words of wisdom:
> Surrendered to the beauty of the world,
> Be stirred with new-enlivened feeling;
> The human 'I' can lose itself
> And find itself within the cosmic 'I'.

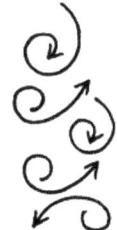

Here the loving, *self-sacrificing nature of Venus* lives in the activity of absorbing something of the light of the world, yet also experiences a state of surrender in which the soul can both lose and find itself. Here, too, the feeling centre of the movement provides the mainstay.

The verse lends itself to a three-way split, albeit with the mode of being remaining the same, but with the soul forms varying according to their role within the verse.

Week 17
Fourth week in July

> Thus speaks the cosmic Word
> That I by grace through senses' portals
> Have led into my inmost soul:
> Imbue your spirit depths
> With my wide world horizons
> To find in future time myself in you.

The inner stance out of which the experience of the verse is recited is that of *Jupiter's wisdom-imbued activity*. The cosmic word enters into the depths of the human soul, filling the spirit with an all-pervading knowledge of union with the universe. The Jupiter movement is rounded, linked to the periphery, and comes to life in the medium of warmth from the midst of the will. Once more the verse is distributed over three eurythmists.

Week 21
Fourth week in August

> I feel strange power, bearing fruit
> And gaining strength to give myself to me.
> I sense the seed maturing
> And expectation, light-filled, weaving
> Within me on my selfhood's power.

The attitude is one of receptivity – inwardly processing what has been taken in, ripening it with light, feeling strengthened within myself. This is the *creativity of the Moon*, a process that receives its impetus and focus from the cosmos, is anchored in the will sphere and concentrated through movement out of the periphery. Here, too, the text is shared between three eurythmists.

Week 26
Michaelmas mood

> Nature, your maternal life
> I bear within the essence of my will.
> And my will's fiery energy
> Shall steel my spirit striving,
> That sense of self springs forth from it
> To hold me in myself.

Nature has ripened in my will, and become the source of strength for inner activity leading to a rich sense of self. This is *the egotistical nature of Mercury*, which senses itself in the core of the soul while also reaching to the realm of the higher self.

This verse is performed by five eurythmists, each with different movements, with a strong central figure surrounded by two others on each side, who are either directed to nature outside or to the human will.

12. THE SEVEN MODES OF THE I AS ARTISTIC EXPRESSION

Week 41
Second week in January

The soul's creative might
Strives outward from the heart's own core
To kindle and inflame god-given powers
In human life to right activity;
The soul thus shapes itself
In human loving and in human working.

The creative soul strives to ensure that divine energy is working effectively both when taking a hold of the self and also in our daily lives. These are the *aggressive Mars forces in the will,* which needs to be applied whenever an artistic form is fashioned. Here too, there are five eurythmists, with one central figure interacting with two other pairs.

Week 43
Fourth week in January

In winter's depths is kindled
True spirit life with glowing warmth;
It gives to world appearance
Through forces of the heart, the power to be.
Grown strong, the human soul defies
With inner fire the coldness of the world.

With the forces of Saturn, our spiritual nature is warmed within, leading to warmth of heart which defies the coldness of the outside world and inflames it with the fire of the soul. The attitude of the I is to express the essence of *Saturn's deep contemplation* and connection to the spirit.

These seven verses from the *Calendar of the Soul* are intended merely to serve as illustrations of the seven modes of the I. Taken together, and including the soul forms, the weekly verses represent a wonderful work to which we shall return in Chapter 16. It is quite natural that the Jupiter, Venus and Mercury qualities are represented more often in these verses than those of the other planets.

Five twentieth-century poems as examples

We shall now turn to some twentieth-century poetry, where the language of the consciousness soul demands the work of the I on the soul in a eurythmy performance. Initially it can only be a matter of listening carefully to what lies behind the words to detect the aspect of the I underlying them.

The source of movement – whether radiating or spherical – is grasped from the structure of the text, and is then given form in eurythmy through motifs, phrasing and word images. Rather than just lending slight colour to the gestures, this is actually the ground upon which they assume their form. It is a matter of comprehending how the I stands in relation to each created form out of the wellspring of each mode, without making an actual planet gesture visible in eurythmy.

Die Menschen (Human Beings)
Rose Ausländer

| Immer sind es | *It is always* |
| die Menschen | *the human beings* |

| Du weisst es | *You know that* |

ihr Herz	*their heart*
ist ein kleiner Stern	*is a little star*
der die Erde	*lighting up*
beleuchtet.	*the earth.*

Here the periphery beams towards the centre point and back towards the outside. This demonstrates the qualities of the Sun – the expression of the whole human being.

12. THE SEVEN MODES OF THE I AS ARTISTIC EXPRESSION

Nicht müde werden (Not to tire)
Hilde Domin

Nicht müde werden	*Not to tire*
sondern dem Wunder	*but to the miracle*
leise	*gently,*
wie ein Vogel	*as if to a bird,*
die Hand hinhalten.	*hold out your hand.*

Talking to yourself as if from the outside, with devotion, respect and inner openness – that is Venus, the attitude of loving self-sacrifice.

Mittelpunkt (Centre)
Rose Ausländer

Welcher Stern	*Which star*
ist Mittelpunkt	*Is centre*
des Himmels	*of the heavens*
Erde	*Earth*
nicht du	*not you*
Aber du	*But you*
Mensch	*O man*
bist Mittelpunkt	*are centre*
der Erde.	*of the earth.*

To be the centre of the universe – you, a human being, are the centre of the earth. Here Mercury speaks, expression of a centred, egotistic being.

Unermüdlich (Tireless)
Rose Ausländer

Untergegangen	*We went*
sind wir	*down*
mit den Göttern	*with the gods*
Wir werden	*We shall*
auferstehen	*rise again*
mit Göttern	*with gods*
sterngeübt	*imbued in stars.*
Ich werde nicht	*I shall not*
müde	*grow tired*
zu sterben.	*of dying.*

Gods and humans join in descending and ascending together in a self-renewing cycle. This is the wisdom-imbued activity of Jupiter.

Unendlich (Infinite)
Rose Ausländer

Vergiss	*Forget*
deine Grenzen	*your borders,*
wandre aus.	*emigrate.*
Das Niemandsland	*No-man's land,*
unendlich	*infinite,*
nimmt dich auf.	*receives you.*

Spiritually at home in a spherical space, it passes through darkness to reach a familiar realm. The Saturn perspective of deep contemplation is one of openness to the spirit.

These examples should suffice to feel our way into what is intended; it is a good idea then to choose our own. Over time we develop an instinct for the poet's approach within the language used. The poet's biography can also shed useful light – get to know the person, was Rudolf Steiner's constant advice. It is the breathing of the I within the words, to which we listen. This gives eurythmists an inner connection to and understanding of the specific situation the poet is in, and belongs to their artistic resources.

Part II

13
Zodiac Gestures as Aspects of the Astral Body

The zodiac gestures and the relationship between sounds and colours have been described in great detail in my book *The Zodiac Gestures in Eurythmy*. In the current context, the emphasis is on how these twelve gestures present facets of soul life. We can then see that they are also ways of expressing the soul's connection to the sense-perceptible, social and spiritual worlds, which is clearly what Rudolf Steiner referred to as 'the second chapter of eurythmy'.[1]

There, in the introduction to the cosmic verse of the twelve moods, Rudolf Steiner spoke of the harmony between human existence and activity and that of the world. he describes the twelve static and seven moving gestures as the 'second chapter of eurythmy'. They become ways of enlightening us on supersensible human nature and of the essence of the soul and the I. Through circumstances it lay dormant until July 1924 when Rudolf Steiner took it up briefly in the tenth lecture of the Speech Eurythmy Course. Here Rudolf Steiner stressed at the very outset that, prior to this moment, eurythmy had arisen from the utterance of sounds in speech, but that he now wanted to choose a new starting point. Forms and potential for movement should now be discerned in, and developed from, the human nature itself. Whatever can be extracted from the human organism needs to be taken back to sounds.

From feeling to thinking and from feeling to action

The qualitative core of the zodiac is Leo, the Lion, with the gesture that connects the heart realm and the peripheral space above and behind it to the higher self. It is the expression of 'burning enthusiasm' between our feeling within the body and the spirit in the periphery. Human beings experience this while asleep, when the soul and the I are dispersed beyond the body into the spiritual world.

Let us now turn our attention to the process of awakening in four stages of transformation. The gesture of 'enthusiasm' as an aspect of the astral body, can lead us in moments of quiet reflection to uncover our mission and ideal as a basis for ongoing practice and work in eurythmy. The soul can emerge from a state of pure feeling in the periphery to one of understanding in a concentrated centre in four ever-changing steps in time.

With Virgo's gesture of 'sober reasoning', the soul retreats back into the body. Secondly, at the edge of the body, 'soberness' arises within the soul. In the third stage, the arms send a radiating movement out into the world like the instant when we open our eyes on awakening and take in the space before us. Originating from the I, the gesture is largely symmetrical, wide awake, feeling the way through all the concomitant connections. We arrive at the 'weighing up the prerequisites of thought' of Libra, the Scales. The fourth step takes us to 'understanding and common sense' of the Eagle that has become Scorpio. The downward-raying gesture points to an understanding of the world, yet within that is expressed a feeling of antipathy that breaks the link between subject and object. We have now arrived at the selective concept that the I creates with the astral body as its instrument. The content of the world arises in me, while its manifestation is outside.

We have just undertaken a journey in four stages, from a comprehensive spirit-soul experience of the periphery to a contracted focal point of thinking in the sense world.

The other aspect of Leo is a process that takes place in space, again in four stages, culminating in 'human action'. Taking our point of departure once more in the paradisal place where I and astral body are united in Leo, the astral then retreats to the edge of the etheric inside the thorax. The gesture for Cancer, the Crab, denotes enclosing and withdrawing back into the physical body. The response of the soul to being held back inside is the 'impulse to action'. It is a spatial process in that the soul is restrained between front and back as it breathes in, leading to the impulse to act.

In the third step, the shoulder girdle is strongly contracted symmetrically giving rise the gesture for 'capacity for action'. The formative force of the astral body that has been mastered expresses itself in the gesture. The soul has grounded itself, overcoming its bilaterality. Gemini, the Twins, demonstrate the ability to create a relationship between left and right.

The fourth step amounts to the realisation of the deed. The will, which rises asymmetrically in a spiral motion, results in a gesture guided by the I and shaped by the astral. Volition as a deed places itself in the sense world, guided from the future and the periphery. The energy of Taurus, the Bull, makes itself known here, vigilant in its surroundings and slumbering when turned in on itself. The soul grasps the vertical dimension as the third direction in which it can be active with physical body through the etheric.

In this way, the entire human soul life is taken hold of and involved, from feeling to understanding, and from feeling to action.

These seven forces give birth to the soul in its totality on earth. What in former times was mystery-school training, is now the education of children in school, with the process in time leading inwards to understanding and the process in space leading outwards to actions. These are the twin abysses faced by the soul nowadays, but this is also the beginning of the freely chosen path of inner training.

The inner and outer threshold of the soul

Understanding the rift between subject and object – a quality of Scorpio – calls forth the inner activity of interest in the world. The motivation for this grows within and turns into resolution, but is not a process to be taken for granted. We need to learn to acknowledge the consequences of our insights, though our everyday habits work against that. It marks the step from what is temporal to what is *beyond space* – the threshold from inner to outer.

The other aspect is to recognise the threshold *after* the action. We are focused and awake to the external object and in our actions, but are asleep within ourselves. This step from the purely spatial to what is *beyond time* has to be achieved. After an action there needs to be reflection, a standing back to review it with the karmic consequences in mind. This moral step demands a great deal from us, in that it implies judgment and criticism. Can I remain steadfast and stand by my action, whatever the outcome?

It is not hard to see that these are the two trials of the threshold of our times, which also generate all our current social and cultural problems.

In the following we shall look at five soul forms, of which the central third one always holds the balance between the soul qualities. This principle can be applied to every action and thought, as well as to the great tasks of destiny in each of our incarnations.

Three stages of attaining harmony within the soul forces

In our bid to discover the transition from understanding to making a resolve, we need to take our interest in an object beyond space and let go of this focal point in order to reach motivation. This process has to pass through a sense of wonder: our gaze warms and matures into resolve or decision. In Sagittarius, the Archer, the soul directs its attention to the world outside with the firm intention to be active.

The gesture of Capricorn, the Goat, shows the impulse to make overtures towards the world and at the same time to test through the will whether the resolve measures up to the situation. This is the 'engagement of thinking with the external world'. In an everyday context, we can only hope to achieve the best possible compromise here.

This situation only comes to a state of active equilibrium and harmony in Aquarius, the Waterman. The only gesture that is always in motion, it oscillates between the source of intention at the root of the nose and the seat of the will in the solar plexus, coming to a balance at the feeling centre where the two streams meet. A state of harmony comes about when the etheric and astral bodies are interwoven and balanced. Hence the epithet for Aquarius is the 'expression of the whole human being', an equilibrium between thinking and action acquired in a state of freedom.

The figure opposite summarises this.

13. ZODIAC GESTURES AS ASPECTS OF THE ASTRAL BODY

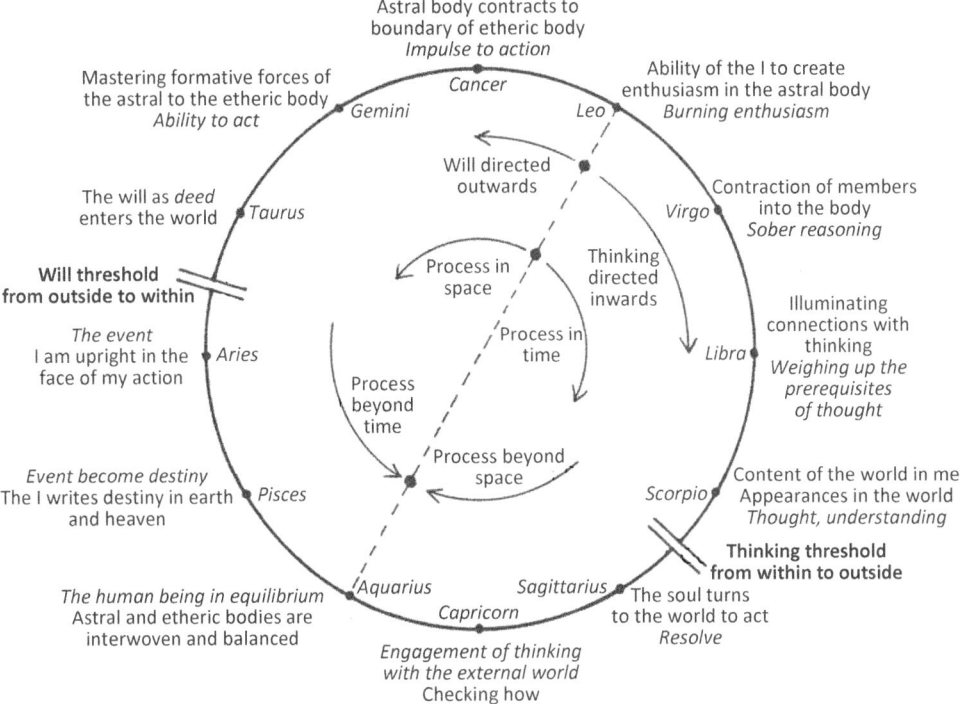

If we search for the transition from action to event, it is to be found beyond time, when we distance ourselves from the action. The review allows us either to examine the necessity of an event or the guilt and regret of an unfinished action. Anything carried out in the world is to be viewed as actively creating the event: the upright human being comprehending the ultimate event and deed for humanity, the Mystery of Golgotha. Aries, the Ram, looks back, reviews.

Finally in Pisces, the Fishes, the event becomes destiny. In bearing the consequences of my actions and wishing to compensate for them, a new impulse arises. The I inscribes destiny into the earth and heaven. The eurythmy gesture points upwards and downwards with the consciousness of a life before birth and after death.

This, too, finds its balance within the gesture for Aquarius, depicting forces in a state of equilibrium moving evenly between light and darkness. When looking back, it represents the need for a new incarnation to find the central point in one's own biography.

14

The Twelve Soul Forms as Artistic Expression

The sources of movement of the three soul forces

Just as with the seven attitudes of the I, it must also be possible to implement the soul forms without actually allowing the gestures to appear directly. We have noted that the modes of being of the I can be expressed relatively easily by the body through a corresponding inner attitude, allowing them to appear through their respective centres of the gesture – the source of the movement – in a spherical or radial form.

The gestures for the soul body are peaceful, with feeling originating in the heart realm. Gestures of directed thinking spring from a centre between the eyebrows. Gestures of action have their centre in the solar plexus. With the 'balancing of the soul forces' in Aquarius, the gesture is bounded by the sources of thinking and will above and below, whereas that of feeling lets the gesture flow freely.

The dynamic sources of other soul forms

On this basis, the sources from which the intermediate soul forms arise can be found as points of dynamic impulse.

If we follow the same order as before, from feeling in the heart realm of Leo to sober rationality in Virgo, then the area of the larynx becomes the equivalent source for movement. With Libra, the corresponding impulse can be located in the region of the cheekbones, ending with the intense focus associated with Scorpio located on the forehead between the eyebrows. In four steps we have progressed from the heart region and feeling to thinking, finding its dynamic impulse in the forehead.

On the path leading to action, we start once more at the heart and Leo and arrive at Cancer, with the dynamic impetus held back in the chest area. In Gemini, the gesture is supported dynamically by the diaphragm and ends with Taurus giving expression to the deed within the solar plexus. Thus with the path leading to action, the dynamic starting point drifts downwards from the heart of feeling to the solar plexus.

In the transition from understanding (with its mainspring in the forehead) to resolve or decision, the impulse to movement sinks down to Sagittarius at the shoulder girdle. In the 'engagement of thinking with the outer world' in Capricorn, the whole of the chest region is gripped and filled with breath. Aquarius' 'forces in equilibrium' permeates the entire human form right down to walking.

In the transition from action to event, the 'whole human form is held from below' in becoming upright in Aries. With the 'event becoming destiny' the dynamic impulse goes 'upwards and downwards through the body' in Pisces, and comes to a 'forces in equilibrium' streaming through the body in Aquarius.

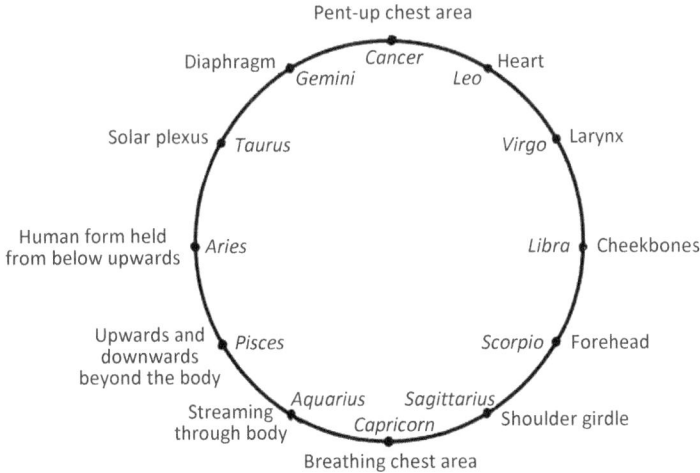

The intentional or dynamic approach in totality

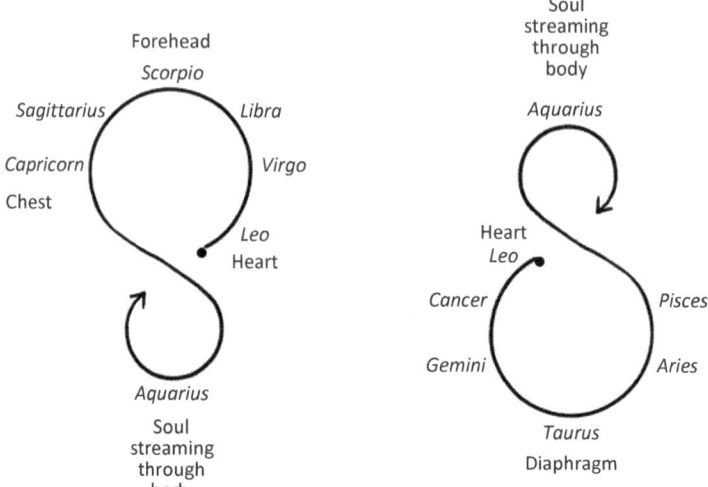

15

The Soul Forms in Walk and Gesture

Just as the seven ways of being as artistic elements include many more linguistic correlations for the expression of the I, so, too, do the twelve soul forms embrace motifs and sentences that reflect the rapidly shifting moods of the soul's relationship to the world. With the seven modes of being, one or other of the three soul sources of movement provides the foundation for, and determines how, our physical form is borne by the I. On the other hand, the kind of walking and the position of the body are an aid with the twelve zodiac gestures in creating a mood anew. For instance, 'burning enthusiasm' is carried out with light foot movements and a bright joyful spirit, directed upwards and behind, with the formed sound likewise radiating up into the surroundings. The gesture for thought, by contrast, is directed downwards, with a posture of antipathy in the back and concentration in the forehead. The shape of the sound is mostly full of character, restrained and targeted. 'Sober reasoning' stays in the part of the body that is contracted – the neck. The human figure seems confined and the sound form is measured. The 'capacity for action' has a firm, steady tread, is conscious of its ability in the shoulder region, receives inner support from the diaphragm and emphasises control of the right-left quality in the sound formation. 'Action' grasps out of the periphery from below and upwards, holds itself firm in the solar plexus, shielding the head and larynx, enters forcefully into the outer world with the shaped sound without being conscious of itself.

The human form is gripped from top to bottom in the 'event', evincing uprightness. It is the most powerful force of them all – a red gesture that shines upwards beginning in a symmetrical double spiral from below. The right hand, arrested in a gesture touching the chin, gives an air of reflection. The sound gesture, too, depicts restraint in the vertical and contemplation as a mood.

The human figure in motion experiences an expansion beyond itself upwards and downwards in the 'event becomes destiny'. Being open to the forces from the periphery, there is a tentative quality of feeling one's way, also in the gesture.

The soul finds its place in the body with the breathing rhythm that maintains equilibrium in the step and the gesture in the 'forces in equilibrium' that is Aquarius.

These hints should suffice to enable us to develop an intuitive understanding of a specific form. Here too, it is a question of feeling our way towards a sense of how the soul links to the world in – or better still, behind – the language.

16

The Soul Forms in Artistic Composition

In a bid to enter into the nature of the relevant soul moods, we shall start with the *Calendar of the Soul* verses. We shall take the same verses and poems as before in order to experience the variety of artistic means used and to comprehend them through listening.

The *Calendar of the Soul* verses

Week 1
Beginning of April – Easter mood

When out of world-wide spaces	
The sun speaks to the human mind,	
And gladness from the depths of soul	*burning enthusiasm*
Becomes, in seeing, one with light,	
Then rising from the sheath of self,	*sober reasoning*
Thoughts soar to distances of space	
And dimly bind	*weighing up the*
The human being to the spirit's life.	*prerequisites of thought*

It is a matter of finding an entry and vantage point out of the exercise of contraction and expansion. The soul's perspective needs to be heeded: is it active in feeling, addressed through the will or implicated in perception? We need to feel our way into this, in order to recognise in which segment of the twelve forms the language is moving.

The overall expression of the I in the verse is that of the whole human being. The soul is absorbed into and united with the light of the surroundings. That is the first motif of 'burning enthusiasm'. This is then accompanied into the distances of space by thoughts arising within the mood of 'sober reasoning' in the second motif. Next, the soul is bound up in a muted way with the periphery in the 'weighing up the prerequisites of thought'. The verse lives in a segment that is on the path from feeling to understanding.

Clearly this needs to be first tentatively felt through line by line, then some motifs can be differentiated like a choir of mixed voices. Finally, the creation of the sound gesture can be made to follow the sequence of the moods, or to carry a quality through according to its function.

Week 11
Third week in June

	weighing up the prerequisites of thought
In this the sun's high hour it rests	
With you to understand these words of wisdom:	*- thinking*
Surrendered to the beauty of the world,	
Be stirred with new-enlivened feeling;	*burning enthusiasm*
The human 'I' can lose itself	
And find itself within the cosmic 'I'.	

In June the soul breathes out into the cosmic realms of space and light, but is just able to hold onto itself within the light of the sun and think. Here the verse changes direction within the same segment. The I now generates loving devotion and the soul weighs up, and then recognises, the beauty of the world in the sun's high hour in a spirit of burning enthusiasm.

Week 17
Fourth week in July

Thus speaks the cosmic Word	*- burning enthusiasm*
That I by grace through senses' portals	*- sober reasoning*
Have led into my inmost soul:	*- weighing up ... thought*
Imbue your spirit depths	*engagement of thinking*
With my wide world horizons	*with the outer world*
To find in future time myself in you.	*- forces in equilibrium*

In July, the cosmic word streams from the light and warmth of the world towards the human being in 'wisdom-imbued activity' and 'burning enthusiasm'. The senses that belong to 'sober reasoning' guide it to the depths of the soul, together with the process of 'weighing up the prerequisites of thought'. There then follows an 'engagement of thinking with the outer world' that will result in a 'balance of soul forces'.

Here the aspect of the whole that discerns and perceives is addressed, but is led to a state of future harmony in a series of leaps.

Week 21
Fourth week in August

I feel strange power, bearing fruit	*- burning enthusiasm*
And gaining strength to give myself to me.	*- sober reasoning*
I sense the seed maturing	*weighing up pre-*
And expectation, light-filled, weaving	*requisites of thought*
Within me on my selfhood's power.	*- resolve*

This verse lives in a medium of 'creative ability', absorbing 'burning enthusiasm', then coming to itself in 'sober reasoning'. Finally it turns slightly to the inner light in the 'weighing up the prerequisites of thought', that guides us to 'resolve'.

Week 26
Michaelmas mood

Nature, your maternal life	*deed*
I bear within the essence of my will.	
And my will's fiery energy	*event*
Shall steel my spirit striving,	
That sense of self springs forth from it	*- event becomes destiny*
To hold me in myself.	*- forces in equilibrium*

With the Michaelmas mood, the language used takes on a more active character. Nature is experienced in the will and in 'action' through the influence of the 'egotistical being'. Actions then lead to the 'event'. The consequence is the 'event becomes destiny' which, refined in the environment of the 'forces in equilibrium', finally becomes capable of bearing the I within. This process of discovery clearly only has words and concepts to describe it, but it needs to be sensed within the language itself.

Week 41
Second week in January

The soul's creative might	} - *impulse to action*
Strives outward from the heart's own core	} - *capacity for action*
To kindle and inflame god-given powers	} - *action*
In human life to right activity;	
The soul thus shapes itself	} - *event*
In human loving and in human working.	} - *event becomes destiny*

In this verse, the 'capacity for aggression' is at work, highlighting the fact that all the soul forms in this verse favour the active side of our nature. Starting at the 'impulse to action', the soul strives towards the 'capacity to act', and finally arrives at the action itself. Then there is a moment of reflection with regard to the 'event' and its repercussions in the 'event becomes destiny'. While it is not always the case that moods can shift from line to line, it applies here, and is often true in Rudolf Steiner's verses.

Week 43
Fourth week in January

In winter's depths is kindled	} *weighing up the*
True spirit life with glowing warmth;	} *prerequisites of thought*
It gives to world appearance	} *resolve*
Through forces of the heart, the power to be.	
Grown strong, the human soul defies	} *engagement of thinking*
With inner fire the coldness of the world.	} *with the outer world*

The inner soul warmth generated by the I provides an ambience of 'deep contemplation' and leads us to the perceiving moral aspect of the soul forms. With the 'weighing up the prerequisites of thought' the verse starts on an intimate note, open to the spirit. The power of 'resolve' increases with the forces of the heart, resulting in an inner fire able to confront the cold of winter through the 'engagement of thinking with world'.

The potential to immerse oneself in three different types of listening – within, between and behind words – can be stimulated by the seven Soul Calendar verses. The opportunity presents itself here to integrate the modes of being of the I in the verses with the soul forms that resonate with them. Both aspects can be seen as qualities in a single eurythmist: around the moving figure and within the gestures interwoven with the surroundings. Patient individual practice is called for here to reinforce the process of making the sound their own on an etheric level. The whole human being appears in a solo performer, while group eurythmy opens up ways to discover new styles of artistic presentation, such as one eurythmist demonstrating the narrative of the piece through speech, while two others produce gestures representing both the ways of being of the I and the soul forms.

Five twentieth-century poems

Now we return to our twentieth-century poems, which can also be cast in this way. Contemporary poetry often strives to express spiritual threshold experiences, often in the in-between unheard spaces. We have to call on our enhanced artistic resources as Rudolf Steiner clearly intended.

Human beings (Die Menschen)
Rose Ausländer

It is always the human beings	} *weighing up the* *prerequisites of thought*
You know that	*resolve*
their heart is a little star lighting up the earth.	} *engagement of thinking* *with the outer world* } *forces in equilibrium*

The mood of the I is the 'expression of the whole human being'. The first motif is a person placed in the world, tentatively 'weighing up the prerequisites of thought'. This is then strengthened by the 'resolve' found in the tension between centre and periphery and harmonised through the 'engagement of thinking with the world', coupled with the 'forces in equilibrium'.

Not to tire (Nicht müde werden)
Hilde Domin

Not to tire	*- sober reasoning*
but to the miracle gently,	*- burning enthusiasm*
as if to a bird,	*- weigh up prerequisites of thought*
hold out your hand.	*- resolve*

This little literary pearl exists entirely in the world of 'loving devotion'. It begins with a gathering of the self in 'sober reasoning', spreads into the surroundings in a state of 'burning enthusiasm', returns meekly to itself in the 'weighing up the prerequisite for thinking', and feels its way cautiously to 'resolve'.

Centre (Mittelpunkt)
Rose Ausländer

Which star	} *duality:*
Is centre	} *event becomes destiny*
of the heavens	} and *resolve*
Earth	} *thought*
not you	} and *resolve*
But you	} *forces in equilibrium*
O man	} and *resolve*
are centre	*- event*
of the earth.	} *weighing up the prerequisites of thought*

Here the mood of the I comes out of the 'egotistic being', but at the same time invokes an ongoing mood of 'resolve'. Starting with a question, everything is then opened with the 'event becomes destiny', and a decisive thought is immediately added, that through the 'forces in equilibrium' man becomes the central 'event'. Then, unexpectedly veering off, ends with the 'weighing up the prerequisites of thought'.

Tireless (Unermüdlich)
Rose Ausländer

We went down with the gods	} *weighing up the prerequisites of thought*
We shall rise again with gods imbued in stars.	} *resolve*
I shall not grow tired of dying.	} *engagement of thinking with the outer world*

The poem operates out of 'wisdom-imbued activity'. Its words lead us into the soul mood of the 'weighing up the prerequisites of thought' as we perish with the gods. Then trustingly we learn in 'resolve' that we are to rise again. At the end we face the moral obligation implied in 'the engagement of thinking with the world'. Is it possible to have a more succinct summing up of death and rebirth?

Infinite (Unendlich)
Rose Ausländer

Forget your borders, emigrate.	} *thinking with antipathy* - *engagement of thinking with outer world*
No-man's land infinite receives you.	- *weighing up the prerequisites for thinking* - *burning enthusiasm* - *event*

The text emerges from 'deep contemplation'. The soul, in wrestling with the 'thought' of breaking down barriers in 'the engagement of thinking with the outer world', is demonstrably unsure of itself in 'weighing up the prerequisites of thought'. It suddenly expands into 'burning enthusiasm', and is roused into uprightness by means of the 'event'. What remains unexpressed between the lines, finds its voice precisely through this dramatic change of mood.

The above examples should be enough to familiarise ourselves with a broader range of artistic elements. They will only become second nature after active practice and implementation. Each time eurythmy is performed, it is beneficial, since the I and soul are in a changing relationship with each other, awakening our interest afresh in the mere watching of it.

A scene from Rudolf Steiner's mystery drama

Maria's speech to Capesius in the third scene of Rudolf Steiner's mystery drama, *The Guardian of the Threshold*, is added to serve as an overarching motif.

The body which belongs to earthly souls	- sober reasoning
bears in itself the means to re-create	} *burning enthusiasm*
the divinely beautiful in noble pictures.	
And though these pictures only live as shadows	- sober reasoning
in human souls, they are the seeds which later	} *engagement of thinking with world*
must flower and bear fruit in world-evolving.	
So through our body we serve the gods.	- *thought*
And the true meaning of his life and soul	- *resolve*
can only show itself to him when in his body	} *engagement of thinking with the world*
the strength of the essential 'I' confirms itself.[1]	

The mood of the I in this speech is the 'expression of the whole human being', interacting with the soul forms in the segment concerned with perceiving and reaching into the supersensible sphere. Maria addresses Capesius, who is holding himself distant from his physical body, in a tone of 'sober reasoning'. She then adds images of divine archetypes out of 'burning enthusiasm', only to return to 'sober reasoning'. Next she indicates the flowers that grow from the seeds in the 'engagement of thinking with the world'. The following line is summarised matter-of-factly with 'thought'. Finally it is made clear with the condition attached to 'resolve' in 'the engagement of thinking with the world', that the physical body will only be able to experience itself intrinsically through the strength of the I.

The true meaning and purpose of the life of the soul can only be fulfilled when the strength of the I is felt in the physical body.

17

Rhythmic Alternation Between the Self and the World

The soul's breathing between centre and periphery

Proceeding from the central feeling of 'burning enthusiasm' of Leo, the zodiacal circle of soul moods can be ordered in two directions: towards either thinking or action. Additionally, there are other processes of the soul-world that are only achievable through individual esoteric training. Within this structure, the soul nature, which breathes quite openly between centre and periphery in Leo's state of 'burning enthusiasm', contracts into thinking and action. It also strives out of inner exertion to expand beyond this into the surrounding soul-spiritual periphery.

This breathing process lies at the root of the spiral and straight-line forces created on the level of the etheric.[1] Wherever the moral and spiritual shaping of the gesture appears – whether tending to the 'event' on the one side of the circle or to 'resolve' on the other – basically the radiating, linear force is at work, but in opposite directions. Beginning at the 'event' there is a simple spiral force, and ending at 'resolve' there is a simple radiating, straight-line force. In this way the seven gestures that relate to the sense-perceptible world and the five belonging to the soul-spiritual realm, can be put in the correct order.

The soul's breathing between symmetry and asymmetry

It is quite possible to discern a rhythmical alternation between a symmetrical gesture and an asymmetrical one on the circle of twelve. Symmetry is the expression of the I taking hold of its inner self, while asymmetry is the effect of the astral body grasping the outer world. Our starting point is once again the 'burning enthusiasm' of Leo, which embodies the most perfect example of the symmetrical double spiral, set against the asymmetry of the double spiral of Virgo's 'sober reasoning'. The 'weighing up the prerequisites of thought' then offers the first simple raying out force and resulting symmetrical gesture, although the placing of the hands one upon the other gives rise to a slight asymmetry. The gesture for 'thought' displays a straightforward asymmetrical linear force from above downwards whereas the one for 'resolve' emanates from a single radiating impulse from behind forwards, rendering it symmetrical, albeit with a mild stress on the right from the inner to outer soul activity. Arriving at the 'engagement of thinking with the world', we have a double raying-out form, from behind forwards, in obvious asymmetry while building a bridge between inner and outer. The mobile gesture that stands for the 'forces in equilibrium' is again a double radiating force working above and below between the three sources of movement, and displays progressive symmetry in the gesture.

If we now take a look at the other semicircle, we move from the symmetrical gesture for 'burning enthusiasm' to the asymmetrical double spiral of the 'impulse to action' that starts behind and in front. with the following 'capacity for action' there is one small a double spiral creating a symmetrical gesture out of left and right; conversely the up-down plane is caught (opposite thinking) in an asymmetrical double spiral in the 'action'.

It is no longer possible to see that the gesture we now have for the 'event' was originally a symmetrical double spiral form, rising strongly upwards in vivid red. The way in which the fingertips touch the chin is reminiscent of the soul mood of devotion. Apart from the impulse to be upright, inner reflection is decisive. A vestige of this quality is seen in the right-hand placed against the chin and pointing upwards.

Next, with the 'event which has become destiny', there is once more a straight-line, radial gesture pointing to heaven and earth that is clearly asymmetrical. Finally the circle is closed with the 'soul forces held in equilibrium' in the power of the double rays of Aquarius.

The whole process summed up in following diagram.

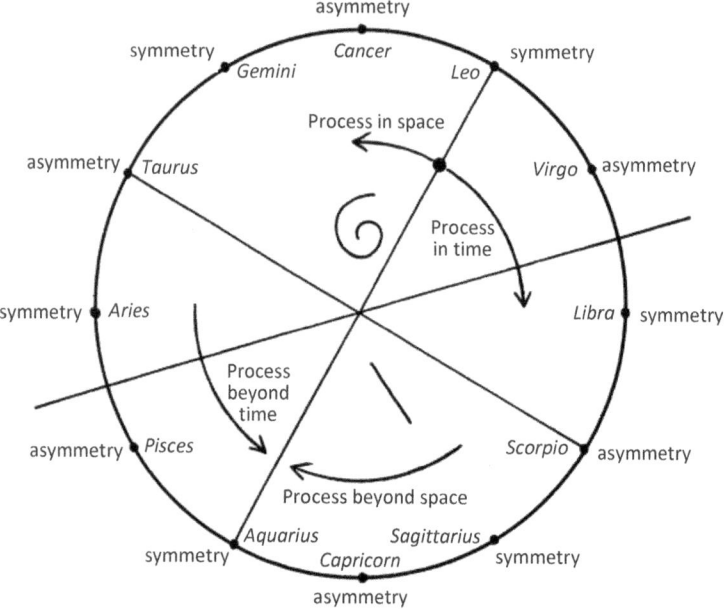

In the upper semicircle (Aries to Virgo) in the day colours, six times.

In the lower semicircle (Pisces to Libra) in the night colours, six times.

From *feeling* the soul strives in four spiral steps into space to *action*.

From *feeling* the soul strives in four steps, beginning in spiral, ending in radial into time to *thinking*.

Then come the five processes that bring us into the soul-spiritual domain:

– from the *event* to the *balance of soul forces* beyond time,

– from *resolve* to the *balance of soul forces* beyond space.

18

Seven Modes of the I and Twelve Soul Forms

This chapter attempts to work out more clearly how the different levels of artistic resources allow the supersensible aspect of the whole human being to appear in eurythmy. Suggestions made by Thomas Göbel over the years of our collaboration, underpin this exploration.

Starting from the Sun's 'expression of the whole human being' as the all-inclusive way of being of the I, we can appreciate how it resonates with Leo's soul mood of 'burning enthusiasm'. In the gesture behind and above the human figure, the astral body is opened wide and receptive to the I. When it moves on to the 'sober reasoning' of the soul, the I withdraws right back into the bounds of the body, but still out of the energy of the 'whole human being', consciousness having been awakened. At the 'weighing up the prerequisites of thought', the I retreats into the head, the 'expression of the whole human being' continuing to be effective. At the moment of total concentration by thinking into a point, the 'egotistical being' shows itself. Subject meets object and understands what is going on in terms of appropriate concepts. The I leaves the centre through its interest in what is outside and finds itself in the object. Thus the I lives in a space of bright consciousness behind the human form in the soul mood of loving, devotion. This link is able to serve as a motif and lead to 'resolve'.

Now human will and 'wisdom-imbued activity' need to intervene and find the best possible solution by the 'engagement of thinking with the world'. This connection is experienced by anyone working in a healing capacity. From here, the 'impulse to action' springs as a soul form radiating in from the periphery of 'wisdom-imbued activity'. Out of the 'capacity for aggression', strength of will, built up by practice and the perseverance of the I, creates the 'capacity for action'. The impact of the 'capacity for aggression' follows in the deed itself. Now the soul is able to be active in three-dimensional space. Cosmic warmth of will then engulfs the head in 'deep contemplation', allowing us to turn towards whatever we have caused to happen. This is the review of the 'deed' that appears as the 'event' in the soul form. If that retrospection includes the motives and consequences of our actions, then the 'event has become destiny'.

The spherical space belonging to 'deep contemplation' lies behind the head. In the Moon's mode of 'capacity for creation', we come via movement at rest to the interplay of the earthly, conscious human being in a cosmic form to the cosmic will-based one in earthly form, allowing the various forces to be harmonised in inner tranquillity. The 'forces in equilibrium' as a soul mood is linked to this way of being.

The state of harmony is summarised in the image below.

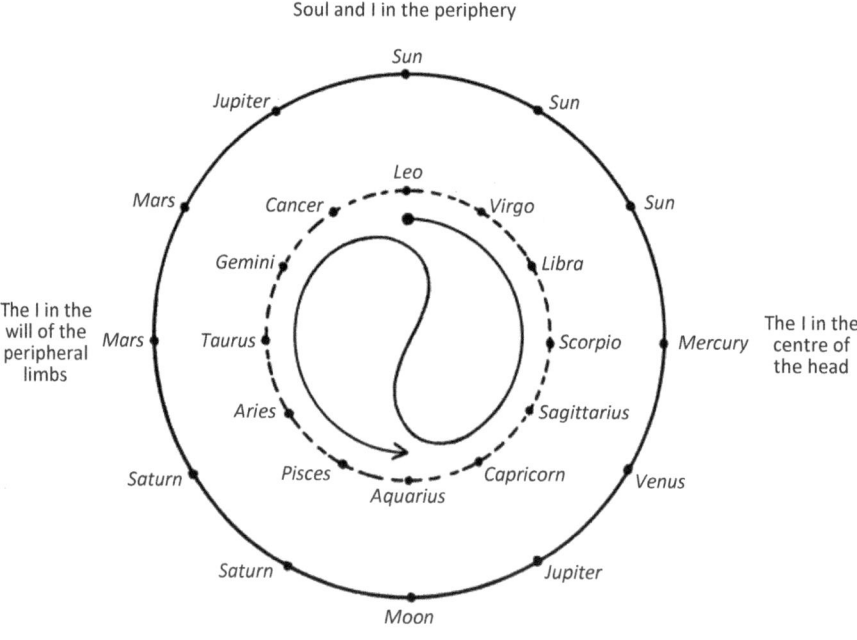

The metamorphosis of the I and its modes suffuse the astral body with the substance it needs to work into the personal biography in space and time, if human destiny on earth is to be properly taken hold of. This particular circumstance poses a challenge when it comes to its representation in eurythmy.

An archetypal picture of the movement relationship between the planets and the zodiac as the totality of cosmic human nature is brought by Rudolf Steiner in a unique way in his *Twelve Moods* verses. This cosmic side of human nature is active in the different parts of the human being when we perceive and work in society. This supersensible human being moulds in the most diverse ways day-to-day life, individual biography, and artistic creations in eurythmy. Alignment with universal laws is taken seriously in the *Twelve Moods*. The order followed by the planet lines in each of the twelve verses highlights the respective mood of each verse.

19

The Whole Human Being and its Counterimages

Just as the archetypal *IAO* eurythmy exercise embodies wonder, compassion and conscience with the forces of Christ, so the opposite can be brought about by Sun demons seeking to strip human beings of their individuality.

In the same way that we have described the soul forms leading to thought through perception, we should also be aware of Lucifer's bid to seduce us through illusion and vanity in our consciousness. Similarly, Ahriman tempts us through endless repetition and the convenience of things in the realm of our actions.

We spoke earlier (in Chapter 13) about the two abysses that are a feature of our times. We lose sight of the role of the I if, on the one hand, we remain blindly stuck in a pattern of action without thought or reflection, and, on the other, if we refuse to look at the real consequences of our thoughts, ignoring our commitment to a binding motif or resolve. The Sun demons, unbeknown to us, have a destructive effect on the etheric body. Nearly all our most recent technical achievements can be ascribed to their influence.

In the last chapter we have dealt with the modes of the I and soul forms in great detail. On this level we live in a decidedly more conscious way, we can wake up to what is asked of us and also train significant parts of ourselves. Yet we can also acknowledge the pitfalls here and mention them in connection with the four main soul forms. The counterimage of 'burning enthusiasm' is fear, which can be mitigated by exercising empathy and forgiveness. 'Thinking' and 'understanding' have their opposite in lying, and can be aided by striving for insight. The opposite of the 'deed' is hatred – the hatred of acting in freedom. Only the love for an initiative can help us out here. From this short

19. THE WHOLE HUMAN BEING AND ITS COUNTERIMAGES

description it should be clear how closely and directly the human being stands within these processes. Even being in a state of 'equilibrium', being healthy and stable emotionally, has the opposite image – someone destroyed and falling apart.

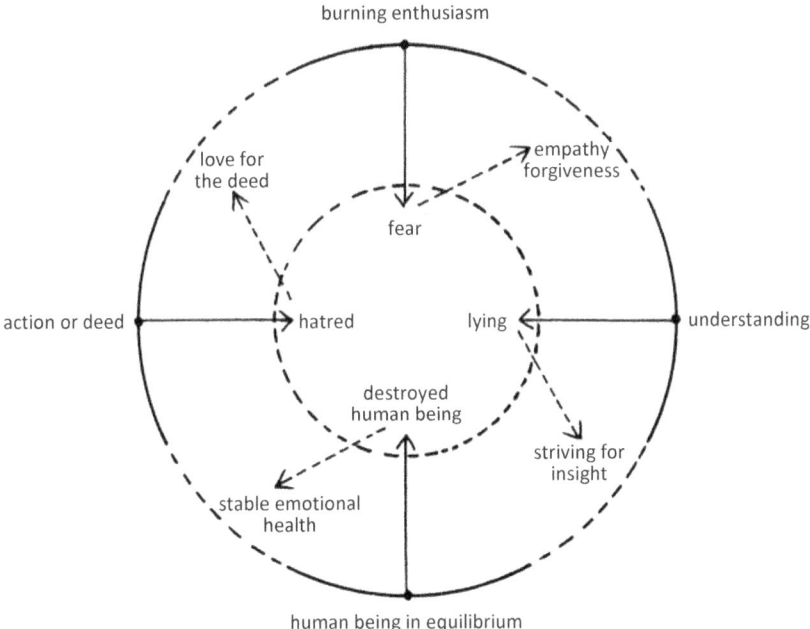

Eurythmy has the task of making the whole of the supersensible human being visible. The training is connected to the laws governing the etheric body, but it is the I that allows the movements to be ensouled. Eurythmy gradually comes to light as the human members are transformed through schooling. The emergence of the invisible human being through the gestures of eurythmy can only be realised when human nature is transformed by selfless devotion.

Part III

20
Planetary Influences and Life Processes

In this third part, additional details relating to the physiological effects of the planets on humans will be described. The individual I, as it becomes involved with all levels of human activity, shows how motifs from the peripheral cosmic forces can serve as a backdrop to the artistic use of the I modes of being.

The following overview highlights the life processes for each planet.[1]

Saturn
    Saturn is the planet of death and resurrection.
    The I manifests in space in the image of a skeleton, and in time in the blood.
    Saturn forces work in the process of incarnation from above downwards from the moment of birth until the age of thirty.
    Saturn operates in the medium of warmth in a differentiating way.
    Blood originates in the bone marrow, condensing in warmth, and disappears into the spleen after three weeks.
    This life process is the foundation for the I to fashion its karma over time.
    In the course of destiny, Saturn draws the spiritual element of the I out of the physical body, resulting in the overcoming of matter by spirit.

Jupiter
    The Jupiter process is that of the sculptor.
    Its forms appear as the expression of the individual's soul.

The forms are all rounded: forehead, all internal organs, the balls of the joints, the brain.

The movement appearing in the gesture is wrested from these forms by the human I, thus giving expression to the soul. This movement is served by the muscles, whose structure gives beauty to the surface of the human body.

The process of the muscles becoming firm and softening, expanding and contracting, is connected to the chemistry of the liver.

Mars

Mars is the carrier of creative, directed movement.

It is the power by which an inner activity is brought into the world and single-mindedly triumphs over it, revealing its essential nature, as in the forming of speech.

Mars forces ray into the body between the shoulder blades. They energise through the iron process in the blood on the one hand and in the process of speech on the other.

Mars processes work in the astral body from within to organise substance.

The one-sided character of Mars forces can be depleted easily through outer activity. To avoid this, the I has to resist the Mars character strongly.

Sun

The life process of the Sun creates a lively interplay of the forces of balance.

The archetypal picture of the Sun's influence is diastole and systole – expanding into space and contracting towards a point – in a spiral motion.

The Sun gathers everything that streams in centripetally, and also sends it out centrifugally into the distance.

It brings about a state of continuous rhythmical interplay between the planetary influences.

There is an equivalent process taking place in circulation, where blood surges forth from the heart into the periphery, returns, flowing slowly at first then faster, in a spiral form back to the heart. As if in miniature, it then circulates within the heart, to be replenished and discharged back into the periphery.

20. PLANETARY INFLUENCES AND LIFE PROCESSES

Venus
- Venus processes are hidden; they need to be discovered intimately.
- The effects are in the depths of the building-up forces where, for instance, substances are taken up and used in the life processes.
- Venus creates a setting and free space for something to unfold.
- Within the organism, the I needs to overcome the building-up activity by breaking down what has been built up by the life processes.
- The activities of breaking down and secretion withdraw substance away through the kidneys and bladder.
- The kidneys mark the endpoint of the Venus function: they separate dead matter from the etheric forces and excrete it.
- The etheric forces radiate as far as the eyes, giving us sight.

Mercury
- Mercury processes bring about sensitive chaos, undirected movement.
- It is movement that simply flows, adapting itself to every obstacle without any inclination of its own.
- Its activity is found in the lymph fluids.
- Mercury inclines towards asymmetry and is responsible for any unevenness in the face or body.
- Mercury is a realist, adapting to everything and ensuring the continuity of the life process.
- The I stands in the way of this stream of life, creating a spiralling eddy and giving an opportunity for human intervention in new direction.
- The flow of fluids in the body culminates in the glands
- The lung is the only organ that is an inside-out air sac – a sort of negative gland – a modification to adapt to the human fluid system.

Moon
- Moon processes are at work in reproduction and the hereditary stream.
- The Moon's influence is present wherever a new organism comes into being; its domain is growth, maintaining and constantly repeating.

Its boundary is the skin.
The nervous system reflects the outer world, bringing it to consciousness as an inner picture.
The Moon-forces culminate in the brain, the organ they govern.
In this differentiation of connective tissue we have an image of the damming of life processes.
The Moon promotes growth within the stream of reproduction and inheritance, and represses life in the nerve-consciousness pole, allowing the I to reflect.
It swims in the flow of time and awakens in consciousness.

Saturn, Jupiter and Mars encapsulate the incarnation of a living organism.

Venus, Mercury and the Moon nurture the process of primal forms with a nourishing stream from below.

The processes of building up and breaking down belong together.

The Sun is the agent by which we incarnate and then leave the body. The latter event also represents the widening diastole that the Sun uses to point our way after death towards the planetary spheres.

21

The Planets Reflected in Human Life

The effects of the planets in the seven-year life phases

It may be helpful in this context to look at the influences of the planets with regard to different epochs in a human life as set out by Rudolf Steiner.[1] Furthermore, the planetary effects in all life phases are reflected in various typical behaviours that trigger certain strengths and weaknesses. These insights can help us recognise more effectively the characteristics and attitudes of the modes of the I.

The planetary sequence below follows the predominant influence in a given seven-year phase.

From birth until the age of seven, the child comes mainly under the effect of the *Moon*. A particular quality at this age is the unquestioning ability of children to absorb with profound reverence whatever the adults around them exemplify. Quite unconsciously they imitate and internalise what they have seen.

Mercury is at work between seven and fourteen. The body has developed sufficiently that forces are set free to unfold conscious faculties. Children are now in a position to learn, build up memory and expand their creative abilities. Now they turn for guidance to a figure of authority in their environment.

Between 14 and 21, young people are influenced by *Venus*. Now soul forces are set free that enable them to approach the world with interest in order to understand and judge it. The power of love awakens too, with attachment to another.

In the time between 21 and 42, the *Sun* holds sway. The I is now freed from the task of building up the physical body, with a resulting state of equilibrium between the inner self and its relationship to society. People mix with others on an equal footing.

From 42 to 49, *Mars* energies largely predominate. There is a nudge towards the spiritual within personal development. Above all, people have an urge to fulfil their life's mission, overcoming all obstacles. In this period energy is directed most powerfully outwards.

The *Jupiter* influence is at its strongest between 49 and 56. Life has reached its zenith. The personality has been matured by experiences and a state of inner peace attained. The ability to shoulder responsibility has been acquired. Personal initiatives and pursuits are the direct expressions of the spiritual tasks that still need to be performed.

Saturn begins to be active between 56 and 63. Life forces diminish and the need to get involved and complete important undertakings begins to dwindle. The inner life acquires more depth. Outer circumstances quieten down while the warmth generated by memories grows stronger.

Planetary effects and typical attitudes

People who hang on to aspects of the first seven-year phase in later life, can be called *Moon* types. They are unable to free themselves from the activities of their own body. They reject the reality of death forces, and thus allow soul and spirit to be too strongly interconnected, preventing easy interaction with the world. Interest is directed chiefly at their own life processes. The tendency to imitate gives way to the desire to be just like everyone else, with the justification that this is the way it is done. There is barely any deepening and development of their inner life. Their goal is simply to increase material possessions and comfort.

The *Mercury* type retains the driving force that defines the second seven-year period. Such people know how to skilfully carve out a place in life with ostensibly autonomous motivation. However, their actions are based on external authority, such as public opinion or scientific viewpoints.

Characteristics of the third phase show up in the *Venus* type. These people have reactions which are completely guided by their emotions. The free unfolding of their individuality is hampered. They lack self-confidence and self-reliance. Their emotions see-saw between attraction and strong repulsion, displaying strong sympathy and antipathy in all areas of life.

The *Sun* phase, between 28 and 42, is actually the principal one in life. A true Sun quality is rarely encountered and is also only acquired after a great deal of effort. It is distinguished by equilibrium between soul and spirit allied to the ability to give oneself totally to things in the outside world, while at the same time determining things oneself.

The *Mars* character often shows itself long before it comes into its own between 42 and 49. Such people have the tendency to commit all their available energy to each thing they undertake. They carry out every deed with rigid purpose that brooks no impediment. Every utterance is made with the force of the weightiest of proclamations.

Jupiter individuals typically behave as if they had already reached an age somewhere between 49 and 56. They contemplate and evaluate all events calmly, as if having a fully developed spiritual faculty at their disposal. They show restraint, as if viewing everything with mature life experience, seeing the connections and keeping the path clear for something bigger or more distant, to turn up.

The qualities of old age live within people of the *Saturn* type early on. They are already anticipating the years from 56 to 63. Slow to become enthusiastic about anything new, they live in their memories when still quite young, presenting a face of solemn, calm composure to whatever situation they are in.

Strengths and weaknesses of each planetary type

The strengths that we owe to the *Moon* are the mundane, routine arrangements that we stick to daily. If we experience them as part of a life process, then we develop healthy tenacity. The weaknesses come to light when humans give in to processes that arise from the physical body itself, such as desires and drives. Also the inclination to pile up money and property is part of this aspect of Moon forces. The sort of imitation that is a product of our times such as following fashion or belonging to mass movements, can also be attributed to these weaknesses.

Mercury plays a part in all forms of learning and practice, or in working on understanding something new in order to attain greater expertise. There is a danger, however, in becoming a virtuoso or a creature of habit, where development comes to a standstill and occupations become soulless. The virtues of Mercury can turn into weaknesses when we strive for a goal using unscrupulous means, or if we try to gain personal profit with the help of others through mass movements.

The power of *Venus* enables us to rise above the mundane with enthusiasm and wonder, and to derive pleasure from art. We can be passionate about ideals, but also fall into raptures. Symptomatic of our times is a fanatical, one-sided pursuit of a cause, coupled with the illusion that we are doing good, without actually being involved in developing it further; it then risks being doomed. Another weakness is the need at all costs to experience strong emotions, even to circulate powerful rumours that appear to be earth shattering. This can escalate to the point that we can find ourselves in impossible situations of our own making, but actually revel in the emotions that are stirred up.

To enjoy being human together with others is a *Sun* quality, as is taking interest in something burgeoning in someone else and delighting in their particular gifts. Living and striving with others and to carry them with us, even when the going is tough, is the greatest virtue that the Sun model can give us. The negative side can be seen when people place themselves in the spotlight, demanding respect and recognition, but are unwilling to support or give to others.

The strength of *Mars* lies in an unflagging commitment of energy to starting something anew or over and over again, defiantly overcoming all obstacles and resistance. Mars does not rest until the task is accomplished. Mars can also bring vigour and transformation, and even in positive situations, can criticise in order to introduce radical changes. This can also be a destructive force. The flawed side to this type is the dominance and militancy to which others may become victims. Mars can also have a bearing on the power of words, working through suggestion, the misuse of catch-phrases and the sort of sensational language that whips up crowds.

Jupiter's strength is the ability to maintain an overview in all situations, while not losing sight of a connection to the ultimate purpose of everything. This marks out a capacity for leadership to which many can rally. The weakness is shown if someone with strong skills is not prepared to place them in the service of something higher that benefit others. Then a tendency to self-aggrandisement and a reluctance to collaborate can have a crippling effect on the endeavours of others.

Saturn's energies are best placed where important traditions need to be upheld and the spiritual protected, thus maintaining a link to the origin of all things. The weak side is when, in the absence of spiritual content, there is a slide into depression and condemnation of anyone or anything around. Empathy towards others is then a problem as the sense of being at a disadvantage quickly arises. Envy is one of Saturn's more negative traits.

The art of living with planetary forces

The different planetary styles can be used as a key to find appropriate behaviour in a given situation.

The style of the *Moon* is concerned with the careful day-to-day nurturing of the life forces. The foundations of life are created by the implementation and operation of regularity and rhythm. Our inner development is also served by the repetition of exercises and ongoing intensive personal study to prepare the ground for new seeds.

The style of *Mercury* is to offer help where humans live and work together. Everything needs to remain flexible and be permeated by continual interchange. Everyone has particular weaknesses and capabilities that can be deployed for the welfare of the whole to reach the best possible outcome. It is a matter of give-and-take and facilitation.

The *Venus* approach is needed to attain a high point in life. Total devotion and great enthusiasm are called upon to remain open to inspiration of the highest order.

The modality of the *Sun* can assist others in realising a goal in their life by empathising and cherishing the same ambitions, and offering our energy. By genuinely sharing our aspirations, we also allow something of ourselves to live in another; this impulse can be of help when we accept their fate. It can also be taking a difficult step in inner development that can only be made with a great deal of personal strength. Discovering a new path that can be of help to others is a healing benefit of the Sun character.

The tendency of *Mars* is to force things through with great strength. This is right and needed if it serves a higher purpose, and creates a way for it to come about. This calls for pugnacity, wholehearted personal commitment and conviction. Mars forces come to the rescue if something needs to be completed quickly with great effort.

The style of *Jupiter* comes into its own when a community of people needs to be fashioned who work together for a common idea or ideal. An overview of the whole initiative is needed before action is taken systematically and single-mindedly. Once a certain level of completeness has been reached, it is imperative that each person find a place within the whole that suits their talents.

The character of *Saturn* is able to constantly evoke in a spirit of warmth whatever once existed. This is also the case in human relationships, where loyalty is maintained towards others because the moment is brought to mind when they once revealed their authentic selves. Saturn remains faithful to individuals whose inner quality has been recognised, but also looks back in the personal biography at the essential high points and to listen to the voice of conscience. To stay true to the sublime is to preserve at the same time our links with our origins.

These perspectives on how the planets work in human beings are thanks to the work of Frits Julius and his book about metamorphosis. Between 1912 and 1924, Rudolf Steiner gave many lecture cycles on the correlation between the planetary forces and the level on which they work, which cannot be considered here. Only those aspects that serve to deepen our understanding of eurythmy have been taken up in this book. These are the developmental steps that Rudolf Steiner described: the spiritual level of the planetary principle, the soul level of the planetary quality, the etheric level of the planetary processes and the organ-building level of the planetary influence.

Part IV

22
Motifs in Eurythmy Training

The first exercises given by Rudolf Steiner

Seven preliminary exercises are to be found at the beginning of the eurythmy instructions given to Lory Maier-Smits in December 1911 in Berlin and in January 1912 in Kassel that are intended to awaken speech and movement in the individual. In August and September 1912 in Munich, there were the first indications on the 'beings moving in dance-like motion' in the third mystery drama and the octave exercise, which in its seminal role opens the gateway eurythmy.[1] These seven exercises serve as a signpost to orientate the eurythmy practitioner as teacher, trainer or performer. At the same time, they are key exercises with which particular skills can be honed and the basic elements of eurythmy brought to birth. These are, for instance, standing in the centre and sensing the surrounding periphery, walking, listening inwardly to speech movements, and so on. The following account offers aspects of personal experiences with the exercises, of which the instructions are on the first pages of *Eurythmy: Its Birth and Development*.

Exercise one
Stepping alliteration, feeling like an early bard bestriding the coastal cliffs amid the roar and turbulence of storm-tossed waves. We raise ourselves upright, supported and carried on the solid ground of the earth. With firm step we stretch to the full height of our vertical form,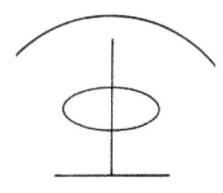
up into the light and the open space of the dome of the sky above us, thereby receiving the strength to conduct an energetic dialogue with the surrounding elements. In our imagination, we can stand fully within the picture of the bard, lifting up our voices with the force of

our breath above the raging elements. Inside us is warmth, above and behind us, light, below our feet, stability, and around us the challenge of relating to the world.

The human being in movement is called upon to find an anchor in the walking step in the centre of the will, in the solar plexus. The upper part of the body closest to the light holds the forehead and surroundings of the head aloft, free in the confidence the I inspires in maintaining uprightness. In between, the feeling centre breathes in and out, connecting the chest and shoulder girdle with the gesture open to the world, paving the way for speech. All three soul forces are called on and addressed in each specific task: the will infuses our step, our uprightness or our relationship to the world in gesture that inclines to speech. With our faculties of thinking, feeling and willing being prerequisites for visible speech, the human being in movement thus becomes receptive to soul content.

Exercise two

Gain a basic knowledge of human anatomy and physiology, especially in regard to movement; look upon the temple of the human body with awe. These are the preconditions which apply to the flexing and stretching of our free limbs, our arms, and our more restricted limbs, our legs.

Our study of the eurythmy step on the one hand, and flexing and stretching on the other, starts here, involving 'using up life-forces' and 'freeing life-forces', a process that is also reflected in the darkening and brightening of the individual aura and the fluctuation of our emotions. When we experience these movements through and through, the process of 'feeling perception' through the limbs becoming a sense-organ for the eurythmist.

In order to acquire an inner awareness of ourselves in movement through the course of the training, whether in respect of a eurythmy element or a form, this activity of 'feeling perception' becomes the foundation for our own practice. In a state of dreaming attentiveness, we are able to sense the whole process of movement, even to alter and correct it during the activity, all the time remaining in the eurythmic flow. We can judge the degree of weight, of light and warmth, of tension and release, of speed or slowness in our movement. Later, intention and awareness of the periphery can be added. All this has the potential to be one of the most important tools for creating subjective-objective forms.

Exercise three

In contemplating Greek sculpture, it is important to experience the form from the inside out in terms of its relationship to heaven and earth, and its relative freedom or limitation of movement. Is the I working from the outside, giving the form the semblance of being earthbound as in the early Greek kouroi or the *Kouros of Tenea?* Or does it seem to be gripped from the inside as in the *Charioteer of Delphi,* or seeking support in the surrounding space with one standing and one free leg, as in the *Apollo Sauroctonos* (Lizard-Killer)? The etheric surroundings visibly play around the figure, as in the *Winged Nike of Samothrace* or the *Poseidon of Melos,* with his expansive arm gesture and open stance.

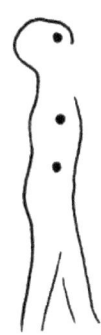

Out of the observation of Greek sculptures, with practice, eurythmy walking evolves. It abhors the sense of being bound to a spot, carries itself forward in fluid motion, and touches the ground with the placing of the feet. The eurythmy step receives its impulse from the will around the solar plexus and its subsequent overcoming of gravity. It is borne freely, given a direction by the focus of thought, and finds contact with the earth as the foot is placed down, completing the action. This action is sensed inwardly by the heart. Rudolf Steiner characterises the sequence of soul responses in the eurythmy step as will-impulse, thought, deed. In the eurythmy step, the feeling wellspring of movement in the soul takes the lead, includes the will-impulse, so that it radiates through the fluidity of the movement, making the eurythmist look as if the ground is not needed for resistance or rest.

The dual nature of any gesture is also addressed by the freely moving centre of the soul (with its quality of both radiating outwards and receiving from the periphery). Even the manner in which the head is held, as if it were part of the space around it, takes on its own expressive language. In this way, the human form can become an instrument for the whole soul in thinking feeling and willing.

Exercise four

This exercise turns our attention inwards, with the intimate task of listening carefully, so that speech dynamics can be transformed into movement, and to hear how different syllables sound the same vowel, albeit framed by different consonants. For example, the speech exercise *Barbara sass stracks am Abhang* is practised from the inside out, with an ear to the intrinsic dynamic of the sounds and whatever accompanies the speech picture rhythmically that could be essential for its forming in eurythmy.

In this way, we can prepare ourselves to hear the sound that a whole poem is tuned to. Eurythmically a crucial factor would be to experience the linguistic shape of a poem, to listen to the sound content and then to sense how the movement could be led through the speech element. If we recite a poem to ourselves in a low voice until the movement body begins to stir and silently makes itself available, we can listen through and behind words, so that ultimately a new creation can arise. The act of listening, involving greater participation in our will-forces, combined with the larynx moving in sympathy with speech, is essential to our perception and comprehension and thus supports the eurythmy movement.

Exercise five

In the first instance, this is a geometric exercise based on the human form. The positions of the six figures of Agrippa of Nettesheim need to be practised singly and subsequently one after the other in a series of swift and light jumps, being aware of the parallel or opposing movements of the arms and legs. It is an exercise designed to master the body, to contract the soul into it, and to draw in the periphery in various ways.

Not until twelve years later does the eurythmy meditation, 'I think speech,' grow out of it.[2] The first three positions anchor the soul, and the other three open it up to the surrounding space, where it strives to find the spirit and connect to itself, while remaining body-bound.

This exercise, a eurythmist's constant companion, brings the central mission of eurythmy to light, which is to build a bridge between the I in the human form and the higher self in the periphery with every eurythmy gesture. When the thought (not the imagination), is resurrected in the will, then 'I think speech' arises as a meditation linking what is sense-perceptible with what is grasped through the soul and spirit.

Exercise six

This exercise involves writing with the feet, creating clear letter shapes in mirror form. A subtle feeling for foot movements and the various ways in which the feet connect to the earth grows out of this exercise. It is clear that the dull sphere of the will which produces stepping and walking is illuminated through this exercise.  The expressiveness of a word is tied up with the steps, leading to the eurythmy forms being imbued with energy.

It is an ancient convention in dance to precede every movement with a step. This moment of awakening in the will through guiding the step is also the bedrock of eurythmy. The effect produced by the shaping of an entire gesture – the authenticity of its execution, identifying with it in the will, its ability to move a spectator – is closely connected to the expressive power of varied and controlled steps. The solar plexus is the source of the movements and takes even stronger hold of them.

Exercise seven

This exercise is connected to ancient circle dances that comprise the first attempt at choral movement. One example involves a circle of several performers stepping round, with each one encircled individually by a second to recreate an archetypal circle-dance of the planets. Another features several dancers moving on two lemniscates whose 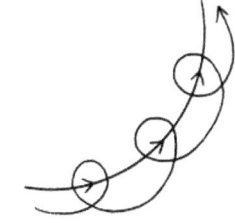 crossing point is the common centre. These were the first choral forms, but without sounds or any other gestures or content. A suitable piece of music would have been added for practice purposes.

The circle dances are centred and are fundamentally geometrical in structure. Group movement in space requires a different type of awareness – the focus is on the periphery.

Six months later, in Munich in August 1912, indications followed for the 'beings moving in dance-like motion to represent the thought-forms relating to the words of Lucifer and Ahriman' (sixth scene in the third mystery drama, *The Guardian of the Threshold*).[3] Three forms were sketched out for each group, whose line-up had to be switched rapidly on a signal, accompanied by vowel-like gestures.

The octave to the seven exercises

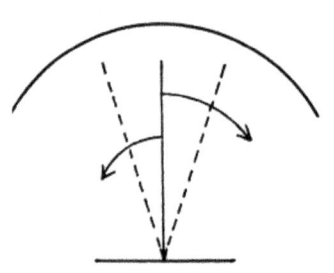

Serving as an octave to the seven exercises, in September 1912 in Munich, the seminal eurythmy exercise, *IAO* on the human form, was added. A type of pillar of light should be experienced as *I* in the upright human figure, extending from the balls of the feet up to the forehead. Next, the body is inclined back – the point on the head is felt behind its counterpart in the feet – to experience *A*. Finally, the body leans forward with the head in front of the feet in *O*. The arms are held close to the body and stay in that position. Eurythmists were also given the additional task of having an inner experience of this shifting of the physical form in terms of colour.

With this, the seeds of the main three soul-sounds were given. The human being poised between heaven and earth, supported by the ground below and surrounded by free open space above, is the very image of *I*. Observing, perceiving and receiving the world, taking it in as if inhaling it, is the picture of a human being standing in *A*; whereas in *O*, the activity is exhaling, surrendering, becoming one with the periphery. The human appears as an I-imbued being in time and space.[4]

The human being is a bridge	*Eine Brücke ist der Mensch*
Between the past	*Zwischen dem Vergangenen*
And the essence of the future;	*Und dem Sein der Zukunft;*
The present is a moment,	*Gegenwart ist Augenblick,*
The moment is the bridge.	*Augenblick ist Brücke.*

The beginning of a verse by Rudolf Steiner, December 24, 1920[5]

The nature of eurythmy as a source of the spirit for humankind was established in this early exercise. The pillar of light embodying the *I*-sound in front of the human form addresses the wholeness of its etheric nature, conditional on the uprightness created by the spine. Within the column of light of the *I*-sound, the point at the root of the nose is touched; the *A* is felt to be held in the solar plexus of the body bent backwards, and in the forward inclination of the *O*, the soul centre is sensed at the level of the collarbone. At the same time, this exercise can only be practised successfully when the pillar of light in the *I*-sound is experienced from top to bottom, with the physical body both accompanying its motion and providing the support when leaning forward.

Thus we have followed a path taking us step by step through the eight exercises to the creation of the ensouled, moving and speaking human being for eurythmy. It is becoming increasingly important nowadays to have clearly in mind what the final aim of each exercise is, as we practise each.

The first exercise leads us from the upright human figure, aware of being placed in the visible world, to the will forces needed to arouse the soul within the body. By means of the second exercise, we arrive at the perception of the body in movement and the breathing gesture. In the third one, we can see how the human form emerges from the entire movement body through motion and how it evolves towards freedom in the walking step, and the gestures connected to the surroundings.

The fourth exercise brings us to a quiet, inner listening to the fluctuation and dynamic of the stream of speech. We can experience that speech heard internally turns into inner movement and learn how to listen behind the words themselves. Through the exercise and its emphasis on the figure of Agrippa of Nettesheim, we arrive at an understanding of the twofold nature of breath. In the sixth exercise, we achieve differentiated expression in the walking step, in eurythmy forms and in speech.

The ancient circle dances that feature in the seventh exercise bring us to choral eurythmy forms, with the striking intermediary stage of thought-forms of Luciferic and Ahrimanic beings.

Finally, the eighth exercise is at once destination and beginning. The human speech faculty is awakened in eurythmy and the self, the I, is conscious of its position between time and space. Many of our fundamental principles in eurythmy grow from this seed.

23
Creative, Formative Processes in Eurythmy

The anthroposophical basis for the breathing of the I

This is best described from the perspective of the I within the picture of the human being given by Rudolf Steiner in the Curative Education Course.[1] Primarily, the focus is on the I, alert and concentrated within the head, and in polarity asleep in the surroundings of the limbs. Between them, in the feeling rhythmic centre, the I breathes in and out in a dreaming state. In daytime consciousness we can speak of the lower I, the ego, and the night-time consciousness of the higher I.

 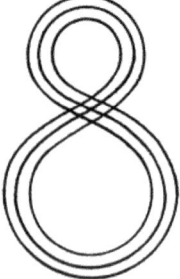

Rudolf Steiner describes how in the head the skeleton is outside, and in the limbs it is inside; conversely, the etheric dominates more on the inside of the head and outside the bones in the limbs. The astral organisation is even more concentrated towards the inside of the head and the outside in the limbs. The I, in image of the ego, dwells with purposeful intensity in the head realm, is contracted in the middle system, and finally, as higher I, spread out in the surroundings in the limb system. Everything is permeated in a breathing way within the rhythmic centre.

The soul forces as an artistic resource

'Ensouled movement' is the foundation of eurythmy, meaning that the I takes hold of the will when we are in motion. Added to this is the living experience of the inner soul, interwoven with the periphery in a feeling, dreaming state. Intentionality then proceeds from the I to capture and sculpt the entire experience and manifest it through the body.

This is a breathing process, embracing all three soul forces, in which the I streams from the daytime consciousness of the lower self, the ego, to the slumbering higher self, the I, in the surroundings. The twofold flow of time in movement is revealed here – the practising that brings us from the past into the future, and the shaping and forming from the future into the past.

The consciousness of the I has the potential to awaken at both ends: to ordinary awareness here, or to over-wakefulness beyond the threshold. It is the mission of eurythmy to wake us up to intuition, inspiration and imagination at this threshold.

The breathing of the I

The soul-spiritual component can only be revealed in eurythmy in the moving form and gesture through the agency of the etheric body. By rousing the sleeping will-forces – through the impulse to shape a sound, through creating a soul form with the body or through expressing a way of being of the I in the posture – the possibility is given to allow these levels of higher cognition to appear pictorially.

Creating forms shaped by the I in the periphery

An effective eurythmy gesture requires that the I is over-awake. That requires a number of preconditions for practice or artistic creation. The basic eurythmy elements need to be held in readiness in such a way that they carry the whole within them, and can bring this knowledge to the practice of the movements. Eurythmy needs the necessary openness to convey the totality from the future directly into the present to enable it to appear.

The actual moment of artistic creation is a threshold experience. Starting at the core of our own inner feeling life, the movement activity then becomes a readiness to receive aspects from the periphery.

This is the moment when the intention to create a form is replaced by surrender to the surrounding space and unites within the over-awake movement. It is then a matter of attentiveness that raises the level of receptivity within our activity and alters the sensation of our movements. With such over-alert consciousness we experience the movement as if led from outside.

Preparing the I for creative activity

What needs to be laid down so that this path to creative activity can be walked unaided? It would go beyond the scope of this book to outline the individual stages of training. They can only be outlined in general, though some quite concrete exercises are described.

At the beginning, everything to do with movement needs to be permeated by the sentient soul and perceived through the feelings. The aim is to create an instrument that enables us to be aware of activity through feeling our own movement organism.

The sentient soul has to be in movement but centred in all parts of the body: feeling at the shoulder girdle and collarbone, willing in the region of the solar plexus and directed thinking in the forehead.

The mind or intellectual soul requires a relationship with the surrounding outer world and through rhythmic exercises and ensouled gestures. The consciousness soul guides the activity that takes place between centre and periphery out of the dynamic breathing of the I.

Gestures that are led by the I are the prerequisites for stylistic work. This is the place at which we can start to grasp eurythmy as a threshold art. It begins to operate on the level of spirit-self when the artistic element is taken hold of by the I in such a way that it appears as the objective channel of expression for spoken or musical offerings.

Exercises that reveal the I in the soul

The I has three key exercises for the soul.

> To lay hold of the instrument of movement purposefully and learn how to master it: by overcoming something.
> To penetrate the soul with breath and feeling in a state of constant mindfulness: in relationship to something.
> To shape the gesture with intent, anticipating its finished form out of awareness of the whole: with regard to something.

The soul has three components visible in the speech process: the will is expressed in speech through the dynamics of breathing and in eurythmy through ensouled movement. Feeling allows speech to resound audibly in the sounding; in eurythmy it conveys its relationship to the periphery in the gesture. The intentionality behind a form can be discerned in the articulation of speech and in the character of a eurythmy gesture.

In connection with speech, the gestures appear in three separate soul manifestations, just as the sound does in terms of movement, feeling and character.

> Movement in differentiated zones.
> Feeling in different parts of the periphery of the sphere.
> Character with differentiated intentionality.

Exercises that reveal the I in the etheric body

The means to practice on the level of the etheric body are self evident – every sound contains the etheric body. We have already given a description of the seven life processes in Chapter 5. We shall refer to them again here without repeating the individual steps.

Attentiveness to all processes as a basic attitude is crucial in enhancing receptivity. We should live, for instance, in a spirit of constant investigation with regard to the principles of movement on the one hand, and to whatever still needs to be created on the other. The perspective from which the artistic form needs to arise, and a more differentiated relationship to it, then begins to take on greater definition. The total picture which first has to be broken down into its various component parts, gradually comes into focus more clearly in the course of this operation as an attitude together with its diverse soul forms. Identification with the totality is a process that can only be carried off successfully when there is analysis on the one hand and the desire to attain the whole on the other.

All these exercises are accompanied throughout by the breathing of the I leading to the formative process. At the same time, dedication to the stream of future time is connected in the periphery to the different levels of being.

Every single artistic method used in eurythmy, from the sound to soul-forms and modes of the I, is carried on the breath of the I, as described in Chapter 11.

24

Exercises and Meditations as a Bridge Between the Ego and the I

Along this path of training the I to live between centre and periphery, we shall make our way once again through the many eurythmy exercises and meditations that have been described. In Chapter 4, the presence of the breath of the I coursing through all the members has already been mentioned as the source of central and peripheral consciousness, so that here the compendium of eurythmy exercises will only be outlined and only their essential features mentioned.

1
The human being, standing upright between heaven and earth, stretches the arms out to the side and moves them from below upwards and down again.

  a) We experience the stretching of the arms and the movement around the body.
  b) We allow the periphery to lead us along the course of the Sun from darkest night-time, through the morning to midday, and then back through the evening to night-time.
  c) We are aware of sleeping consciousness in the lower realm, dreaming consciousness in the periphery and waking consciousness in the upper realm.

A medieval saying on a sundial on a church tower in the southern Black Forest expresses the essence of our three artistic modes of expression:

O you, human being
Language of God
Like the sun,
Pause in the midst
Of your movement.

2

This is the exercise, 'Light streams upwards, weight bears downwards'.[1]

3

The upright human form, standing between light and darkness (earth), surrounded by wind (air) and water, asserts itself with the warmth of the I against the elements (see the alliteration exercise in Chapter 22).

4

The upright human rebels against being fettered to the earth, and steps freely to advance over the ground and rediscover a connection to it. The entire soul is caught up with the will in this exercise (see the walking exercise in Chapter 22).

5

Contraction and expansion is both the archetypal gesture of the ensouled human and of eurythmy (see Chapter 4). The four forms or steps of contraction and expansion that belong to the whole human being have been described. In all these exercises, the principal factor is the I-breath, or qualities that are to be found on every human level when eurythmy is carried out. It is worth pointing out here that any gesture that speaks in eurythmy is always an expression of contraction and expansion and derives specifically from the I. This can be clarified by means of three sound gestures.

B: The sound is generated by the yellow in the figure, the blue that surrounds it and the red in the character. In other words, there is yellow in the expansion of the human form, blue in the contraction gesture and red in the expression of the sound in the character.

I: The overall configuration of this vowel is a yellow-gold lightform with a blazing vermillion red gesture, countered by the light blue contracted character on the other.

L: The silver-grey movement breathes and flows along in a dreamlike state, while the lilac periphery introduces a dynamic and the orange character finally lets the sound appear. This is specifically the case for the central sound of *L*.

These three examples should suffice to show that there is simultaneousness in all the sound gestures. In the sound the whole soul and the I grasp the instrument of the body.

6

A key exercise to use when gathering soul forces to take hold of the body, are the three circles perpendicular to one another whose intersecting diameters form a three-dimensional cross. The centre point is also the source of *feeling* movement of the upright human being. In the vertical plane, we link above and below in the feeling direction. With the horizontal circle the direction of *thinking* joins right and left. Lastly, the direction of the *will* connects front and back in action.

Rudolf Steiner gives four anapest exercises together with some mood indications that bear out their origins in the above description.²

Anapest (˘ ˘ —) with the gesture for *inwardness*. The upper arms are held against the upper body in the frontal plane. The forearms are kept in the horizontal plane with the fingers extending outwards and the index finger and thumb joined in a close circle. Willing and feeling are also held in check in this plane, so conferring an expression of intimacy.

Anapest (˘ ˘ —) with the gesture for *merriment*. A light jumping step is performed, whereby the arms are held out to the side and above and slightly behind the head in the plane of the will. The jump emphasises the upwards direction of the arms towards the feeling and light realm.

Anapest (˘ ˘ —) done *energetically* with a strong emphatic step forwards. The arms are also stretched out in front following the direction of the will, the hands clapping and the intention reaching towards a distant goal.

Tragic anapest (˘ ˘ — —) with the long beat doubled in the tragic anapest, the arms raised from below, staying just under the horizontal as if emotion is bound to gravity. In the second long beat the body is static, but bent backwards in an attitude of lament and sorrow.

The *L*-sound as a consonant gesture connects heaven and earth, overcoming and transforming matter. The seven *L*s in Hallelujah underline the urge of the soul to elevate and cleanse itself in the sight of God, especially when they intensify. The centre of the will is down below in front, and in the upper zone slightly expanded behind. The intention of the meditation is held fast in the sagittal plane that divides left and right.

All three soul-forces have the wellspring of the movement in different places: that of the *will* in the centre of incarnation on the level of the solar plexus, of *feeling* in the seat of the soul where the shoulder girdle meets the clavicle, and for directed *thought or intention,* at the root of the nose or rather the point of individuation above the body.

7

The three archetypal phenomena of contraction and expansion are each connected to a movement source and manifest a soul energy active within the exercise.

The *breath of light* emerges out of directed thought, moving from the surrounding light above the body to below the body into the darkness of the earth.

The *breath of warmth,* emanating from the heart of our emotions, spreads out into the social surroundings, embracing everything warmly, then contracts out of the periphery into itself, insulating itself in coldness.

The *breath of life* exists in the region of the will, in the solar plexus, the centre of incarnation. It is able to contract out of the circle of the will into the very point of death, or to expand and breathe out into the realm of volition.

8

Eurythmy has three forms that express the I in space: The *central* I is to be seen as a point on the standing, upright human form.

The *breathing* I being manifests in the straight line

that on the way back, touches all the points passed on the way there.

The *peripheral* I creates a circle in space that has a clear relationship with its own centre.

The two guiding principles of form come to light here. The straight line or ray, an archetypal image of what weaves between the stars and earth, is an expression of the I in forwards and backwards movement. By contrast, the spiral, an archetypal image of all curved forms, links the peripheral I to the central I living in the heart. This corresponds to the circle and its centre.

9

In 1924, Rudolf Steiner turned the figures of Agrippa of Nettesheim into a meditation on the human form. It became an exercise of the basis of the I as a being of breath. The first three positions relate to the way in which the daytime I relates to visible speech. The second three positions are how the peripheral I relate to the fashioning of the whole tableau, which also embodies the archetypal character of what appears in eurythmy.

10

The *IAO* exercise given right at the beginning by Rudolf Steiner as a meditation on the human figure (see Chapter 22), has the *I*-sound appearing in front of the body as an axis of light, from which the *A* can be experienced when the body is inclined back and *O* when inclined forward.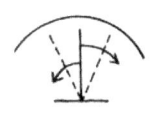

This exercise also has a primordial quality in so far as the I and the soul feel their way into the body between time and space as if coming from far out in the cosmos. At the same time, the essence of the present moment is revealed in *I*-sound, with the past behind it in *A* and the future in front of it in *O*. The *I*-sound is formed from a directed thought as a straight line that connects forehead and the front of the foot. The *A,* sensed behind through inclining back, allows awareness of the incarnation centre. The *O,* leaning forward, encourages perception of the feeling source in its role as the 'guardian'. This ensures that the exercise does not descend into the purely physical.

11

The two key exercises, given originally for various flowing sequences of vowels and consonants to be produced, become the foundation stones for lyric and cosmic lyric poetry.

The spiral forms involved in 'Look into yourself – look around yourself' are carried on the breath of the I in a dreaming, feeling way between myself and the world. The double spiral of 'We seek the soul – the spirit shines towards us', demands a consciously grasped reversal of the position of the will between the centre in front and periphery behind. Rudolf Steiner was excited by the qualitative conjunction of the Euclidean spiral (centre-oriented) and a projective geometry spiral (periphery-oriented), writing next to it, *Vita eurythmo-Geometrie* (long live eurythmic geometry). This is namely the joining of centre-oriented with periphery-oriented forms in the time-space dimension of eurythmy movement. This double spiral becomes the key to all language arising from the consciousness-soul poetry of the twentieth and twenty-first centuries and of Rudolf Steiner's collection of verses and meditations – a language that is always crossing the threshold, with the challenge to bring together the I at the centre and the I in the periphery.

12

The archetypal colour gestures, which were lost for decades, are likewise expressions of the I breath.[3]

Blue, yellow and green as eurythmy colour gestures are created from the feeling centre of movement, from Euclidean space. Blue comes from the sphere, yellow from the straight line, and green from connecting the two. Blue builds up a cloudy gesture arising in the surroundings, yellow, a radiating one from the centre, and green an even, unifying gesture. These fill three-dimensional space qualitatively. On the other hand, orange, red and violet are formed from projective space in eurythmy. The gesture for orange has the twin characteristics of radiating into the periphery and absorbing from it. Red enables the possibility to stand vertically upright from below upwards, with the counterflow from the periphery coming to a point of rest in the gesture, streaming inwardly back as far as the feet. Violet weaves calmly up and down in perpetual motion, guided out of the periphery, controlling gravity as of from the outside.

13

The metamorphosis of the nature of the vowels as a path of incarnation for the I, was described in Chapter 9. Here we simply want to point once more that the five vowels in eurythmy are an image of the breath of the I. The I approaches from the periphery and is compressed in *A*, contracts to become *E*, identifies itself with physicality and the everyday self in *I*, dissolves into the surroundings in *O*, and strives once more to be part of space in *U*, and then the I becomes peripheral again.

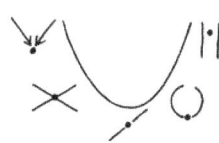

14

In conclusion, we need to look once more at the exercise that Rudolf Steiner called an 'esoteric intermezzo', given to make the eurythmy instrument more flexible – *TAO*. The breathing process of the I comes into the picture once more. With an awakening jolt, the cosmic I draws in the *T* from Leo in the surrounding zodiac. The soul responds with

the double interval of the six and seventh, then breathes the cosmic I into the feeling space of the third, opening up in *A*, and in the interval of the second, the cosmic I unites with the etheric and impresses itself on it in the *O*, which is held actively over time in the gesture.

From the perspective of human development, the *TAO* meditation is the oldest exercise, having accompanied us through long ages and will be effective in the future, precisely in the form that Rudolf Steiner gave for eurythmy.

Just as the *IAO* exercise is the first meditation to feature in the development of eurythmy, so 'I think speech' and the *TAO* are the last to be worked. They all have the principal task of working on the I breath.

15

The verse given as a meditation for eurythmy sums up all that has gone before, in that the forces that emanate from the universe and the surrounding air and light are to be found within the human being. They are also found in the eurythmists borne along by the strength of the I in the time-space dimension and beyond, manifesting as a new divine and human word in step, gesture and intent.

I seek within myself	*Ich suche im Innern*
The working of creative forces,	*der schaffenden Kräfte Wirken,*
The life of creative powers.	*der schaffenden Mächte Leben.*
The powerful weight of earth	*Es sagt mir*
Tells me	*der Erde Schweremacht*
Through the word of my feet,	*durch meiner Füsse Wort,*
The forming might of the air,	*Es sagt mir*
Tells me	*der Lüfte Formgewalt*
Through the singing of my hands,	*durch meiner Hände Singen,*
The force of the light of heaven	*Es sagt mir*
Tells me	*des Himmels Lichteskraft*
Through the thinking of my head,	*durch meines Hauptes Sinnen,*
How the world in man	*Wie die Welt im Menschen*
Speaks, sings, thinks.[4]	*spricht, singt, sinnt.*

Notes

1. Forming the Eurythmy Gestures for the Planets
1 Steiner, *Eurythmy as Visible Speech,* lecture of July 7, 1924.
2 Steiner, *Eurythmy as Visible Speech,* lecture of July 7, 1924, p. 118.
3 Steiner, *Eurythmy as Visible Speech,* lecture of July 7, 1924.

2. The Characteristics of the Planetary Gestures
1 Steiner, *Eurythmy as Visible Speech,* lecture of July 7, 1924.
2 Steiner, *Eurythmy as Visible Speech,* lecture of July 7, 1924, p. 122.
3 Steiner, *Eurythmy: Its Birth and Development,* lecture of Aug 24, 1915, p. 78.
4 Steiner, *Eurythmy as Visible Speech,* lecture of July 8, 1924, p. 124.
5 Steiner, *Eurythmy as Visible Speech,* lecture of July 7, 1924, pp 119, 122.

4. The I as a Being of Breath
1 Steiner, *Eurythmy: Its Birth and Development,* notes of Sep 21, 1912, p. 39.
2 A detailed description (in German) of the processes of contraction and expansion is to be found in Barfod, *Die drei Urphänomene eurythmischen Bewegens,* and Thomas Göbel, 'Das Ich als Doppelwesen' in *Tycho de Brahe Jahrbuch* 1994.

5. Planetary Influences in Prenatal and Earthly Existence
1 Steiner, *Rosicrucianism and Modern Initiation,* lectures of April 21 and 22, 1924.
2 Göbel, Thomas, 'Sieben Seinsweisen des Ich' and 'Ephesische Mysterien, die Kategorien des Aristoteles, das mittelalterliche Rosenkreuzertum und die Eurythmie I' in *Rundbrief der Sektion für Redende und Musizierende Künste,* Easter–Michaelmas 2001.
3 Based on collaboration with Thomas Göbel, see 'Ephesische Mysterien, die Kategorien des Aristoteles, das mittelalterliche Rosenkreuzertum und die Eurythmie II' in *Rundbrief der Sektion für Redende und Musizierende Künste,* Easter 2002.
4 Steiner, *Rosicrucianism and Modern Initiation,* lecture of April 21, 1924, p. 122.

5 Steiner, *Rosicrucianism and Modern Initiation,* lecture of April 22, 1924, p. 135.
6 See Lindenau, *Der übende Mensch,* and Steiner, *Anthroposophy (A Fragment),* and *The Riddle of Humanity.*

6. The Planetary Processes in Varying Sequences

1 This sequence is based on Lindenau, *Der übende Mensch,* and Steiner, *The Riddle of Humanity.*
2 The inscriptions were on a sketch from about 1911 for the original Johannes-Bau in Munich. See Steiner, *Mantric Sayings Meditations,* p. 237.

8. The Seven Levels of Manifestation of the Vowels

1 Steiner, *Eurythmy as Visible Speech,* lecture of June 24, 1924, pp. 34f.
2 A more detailed description (in German) can be found in Barfod, *Konsonanten und Vokale.*
3 Steiner, *Eurythmy as Visible Speech,* lecture of June 26, 1924, p. 51.
4 Steiner, *Eurythmy as Visible Speech,* lecture of June 26, 1924, pp. 52–54.
5 Steiner, *The Alphabet,* p. 2.
6 Steiner, *Eurythmy as Visible Speech,* lecture of June 24, 1924, p. 32.
7 Steiner, *Eurythmy as Visible Singing,* lecture of Feb 19, 1924, p. 41.
8 Steiner, *Eurythmy as Visible Singing,* lecture of Feb 19, 1924, p. 39.
9 Steiner, *Eurythmy as Visible Singing,* lecture of Feb 19, 1924, p. 42.
10 Steiner, *Eurythmy Therapy,* lecture of April 13, 1921, p. 22.
11 Steiner, *Rosicrucianism and Modern Initiation,* lecture of April 21, 1924, p. 122.
12 Steiner, *Eurythmie; Die Offenbarung der sprechenden Seele,* address of July 21, 1923, p. 384.
13 Steiner, *Eurythmy as Visible Speech,* lecture of June 25, 1924, p. 43.
14 Steiner, *Eurythmy as Visible Speech,* lecture of June 26, 1924, p. 52.
15 Steiner, *Eurythmy as Visible Singing,* lecture of Feb 19, 1924, p. 39.
16 Steiner, *Eurythmy Therapy,* lecture of April 13, 1921, pp. 21f.
17 Steiner, *Eurythmy Therapy,* lecture of April 16, 1921, p. 60.
18 Steiner, *Eurythmy Therapy,* lecture of April 13, 1921, p. 16.
19 Steiner, *Eurythmy as Visible Speech,* lecture of June 26, 1924, p. 53.
20 Steiner, *Eurythmy as Visible Speech,* lecture of Aug 26, 1923, p. 176.
21 Steiner, *Eurythmy as Visible Speech,* lecture of July 2, 1924, p. 91.
22 Steiner, *Eurythmy as Visible Speech,* lecture of June 24, 1924, p. 34.
23 Steiner, *Eurythmy Therapy,* lecture of April 13, 1921, p. 21.
24 Steiner, *Eurythmie; Die Offenbarung der sprechenden Seele,* address of July 21, 1923, p. 384.
25 Steiner, *Eurythmy as Visible Speech,* lecture of July 7, 1924, pp. 117f.
26 Steiner, *Man in the Light of Occultism,* lecture of June 11, 1912, p. 173.
27 Steiner, *Eurythmie; Die Offenbarung der sprechenden Seele,* address of July 21, 1923, p. 384.

28 Steiner, *Eurythmy as Visible Singing,* lecture of Feb 19, 1924, p. 40.
29 Steiner, *Eurythmy: Its Birth and Development,* lecture of Sep 16, 1912, p. 25.
30 Steiner, *Eurythmy as Visible Speech,* lecture of June 26, 1924, p. 53.
31 Steiner, *Eurythmy as Visible Speech,* lecture of June 26, 1924, p. 53.
32 Steiner, *Eurythmy as Visible Speech,* lecture of June 26, 1924, p. 53.
33 Steiner, *Eurythmy as Visible Singing,* lecture of Feb 19, 1924, p. 40.
34 Steiner, *Eurythmy Therapy,* lecture of April 13, 1921, p. 21.
35 Steiner, *Eurythmy as Visible Speech,* lecture of July 7, 1924, p. 119.
36 Steiner, *Menschenfragen und Weltenantworten,* lecture of July 1, 1922, p. 62.
37 Steiner, *Eurythmy: Its Birth and Development,* lecture of Sep 16, 1912, p. 25.
38 Steiner, *Eurythmy as Visible Singing,* lecture of Feb 19, 1924, p. 40.
39 Steiner, *Eurythmy as Visible Speech,* lecture of June 26, 1924, p. 54.
40 Steiner, *Eurythmy as Visible Speech,* lecture of June 25, 1924, p. 39f.
41 Steiner, *Eurythmy as Visible Singing,* lecture of Feb 19, 1924, p. 40.
42 Steiner, *Eurythmy as Visible Singing,* lecture of Feb 19, 1924, p. 41.
43 Steiner, *Eurythmy Therapy,* lecture of April 13, 1921, p. 21.
44 Steiner, *Eurythmy Therapy,* lecture of April 16, 1921, p. 37.
45 Steiner, *Eurythmy as Visible Speech,* lecture of July 7, 1924, p. 121.
46 Steiner, *Man in the Light of Occultism,* lecture of June 11, 1912, p. 157.
47 Steiner, *Rosicrucianism and Modern Initiation,* lecture of April 21, 1924, p. 122.

9. The Five Vowels as an Image of Their Nature

1 Steiner, *Eurythmie; Die Offenbarung der sprechenden Seele,* address of July 21, 1923, p. 384.
2 Steiner, *Eurythmie; Die Offenbarung der sprechenden Seele,* address of July 21, 1923, p. 384.
3 Steiner, *Eurythmy as Visible Singing,* lecture of Feb 19, 1924, pp. 40f.

10. The Seven Aspects of the I and Their Soul Moods

1 Steiner, *Eurythmy as Visible Speech,* lecture of July 1, 1924, p. 76.
2 See also collaboration with Göbel, 'Über das Verhältnis der Seinsweisen des Ich zu den Gemütsstimmungen' in *Rundbrief der Sektion für redende und musizierende Kunste,* Easter 2003.

11. The Whole Human Being Appears in Eurythmy

1 Steiner, *Eurythmy: Its Birth and Development,* faculty meeting at the Eurythmeum, April 30, 1924, p. 141.
2 Steiner, *Eurythmy as Visible Speech,* lecture of July 7, 1924, pp. 122f.
3 Steiner, *Speech and Drama,* lecture of Sep 6, 1924.
4 See also (in German) the author's collaboration with Thomas Göbel, 'Eurythmie als ganzer Mensch' in *Rundbrief der Sektion für Redende und Musizierende Künste,* Easter 2005.

12. The Seven Modes of the I as Artistic Expression
1 Steiner, 'Preface to the Second Edition' *The Calendar of the Soul*. This and the following verses quoted are from the translation by Ruth and Hans Pusch.

13. Zodiac Gestures as Aspects of the Astral Body
1 Steiner, 'Planetentanz, Zwölf Stimmungen, Satire' lecture of Aug 29, 1915, in *Wahrspruchworte*, p. 68. See also Steiner, *Twelve Moods*.

16. The Soul Forms in Artistic Composition
1 Steiner, *The Guardian of the Threshold*, Scene 3, in *Four Mystery Dramas*, p. 330.

17. Rhythmic Alternation Between the Self and the World
1 Described in detail in Barfod, *The Zodiac Gestures in Eurythmy*, pp. 25ff.

20. Planetary Influences and Life Processes
1 Compiled from Lievegoed, *Planetenwirken und Lebensprozesse*.

21. The Planets Reflected in Human Life
1 Steiner, *True and False Paths of Spiritual Research*, lecture of Aug 16, 1924.

22. Motifs in Eurythmy Training
1 Steiner, *Eurythmy: Its Birth and Development*, pp. 21f, 34.
2 A detailed description (in German) is in Barfod, *Ich denke die Rede*.
3 Steiner, *Eurythmy: Its Birth and Development*, p. 21.
4 For a more detailed description (in German), see Barfod, *IAO und die eurythmischen Meditationen*.
5 Steiner, *Wahrspruchworte*, p. 143.

23. Creative, Formative Processes in Eurythmy
1 Steiner, *Education for Special Needs*, lecture 5 of June 30, 1924.

24. Exercises and Meditations as a Bridge Between the Ego and the I
1 Barfod, *IAO und die eurythmischen Meditationen*.
2 Steiner, *Eurythmy: Its Birth and Development*, notes of Sep 19, 1912, p. 32.
3 See also Barfod, *The Zodiac Gestures in Eurythmy*, pp. 17ff.
4 Steiner, *Eurythmy as Visible Speech*, lecture of July 11, 1924, p. 152.

Bibliography

Barfod, Werner, *IAO und die eurythmischen Meditationen,* Verlag am Goetheanum, Switzerland 2016.
—, *Ich denke die Rede: Leitsatzübung der Eurythmie,* Verlag am Goetheanum, Switzerland 2020.
—, *Konsonanten und Vokale – R. Steiners Charakteristika für die Eurythmie,* Sentovision, Switzerland 2014.
—, *The Zodiac Gestures in Eurythmy,* Floris Books 2019.
—, et al. (eds.) *Die Drei Urphänomene eurythmischen Bewegens,* Verlag am Goetheanum, Switzerland 1996.
Julius, Frits H. *Metamorphose: ein Schlüssel zum Verständnis von Pflanzenwuchs und Menschenleben,* Mellinger, Germany 1984.
Lievegoed, B. *Planetenwirken und Lebensprozesse in Mensch und Erde,* Freies Geistesleben, Germany 1992.
Lindenau, Christof, *Der übende Mensch,* Freies Geistesleben, Germany 2001.
Steiner, Rudolf. Volume Nos refer to the Collected Works (CW) or to the German Gesamtausgabe (GA).
—, *The Alphabet: an Expression of the Mystery of Man,* Mercury Press, USA 1982.
—, *Anthroposophy (A Fragment)* (CW 45) Anthroposophic Press, USA 1996.
—, *The Calendar of the Soul,* tr. by Ruth and Hans Pusch, Anthroposophic Press, USA 1982.
—, *Eurythmie; Die Offenbarung der sprechenden Seele* (GA 277) Steiner Verlag, Switzerland 1999.
—, *Eurythmy as Visible Singing* (CW 278) Rudolf Steiner Press, UK 2019.
—, *Eurythmy as Visible Speech* (CW 279) Rudolf Steiner Press, UK 1984.
—, *Eurythmy: Its Birth and Development* (CW 277a) Anastasi, UK 2002.
—, *Eurythmy Therapy* (CW 315) Rudolf Steiner Press, UK 2009.
—, *Education for Special Needs* (CW 317) Rudolf Steiner Press, UK 2015.
—, *Four Mystery Dramas* (CW 14) tr. by Ruth and Hans Pusch, SteinerBooks, USA 2014.
—, *Man in the Light of Occultism, Theosophy and Philosophy* (CW 137) Rudolf Steiner Press, UK 1964.
—, *Mantric Sayings, Meditations 1903–1925* (CW 268) SteinerBooks, USA 2015.

—, *Menschenfragen und Weltenantworten* (GA 213) Steiner Verlag, Switzerland 1987.
—, *The Riddle of Humanity* (CW 170) Rudolf Steiner Press, UK 1990.
—, *Rosicrucianism and Modern Initiation* (CW 233a) Rudolf Steiner Press, UK 2020.
—, *Speech and Drama* (CW 282) Anthroposophic Press, USA 1984.
—, *True and False Paths of Spiritual Research* (CW 243) Rudolf Steiner Press, UK 2020.
—, *Twelve Moods,* Mercury Press, USA 1984.
—, *Wahrspruchworte* (GA 40) Steiner Verlag, Switzerland 2005.

Index

A (vowel) 39
— and metamorphosis of the I 50
— and soul moods 52f
—, stages of manifestation 42f
— and Venus 22
aggression, capacity for (expression of Mars) 17, 63
Agrippa of Nettesheim, figures of 116f, 119, 129
Ahriman 96
anapest exercises 127f
anatomy and physiology 114f
Aquarius 74–78, 92, 94
Aries 36, 75, 77f, 92, 94
Artemis 34f
astral body 56f, 93–95
— and zodiac gestures 71–75, 79
—, dual nature of 23
asymmetry and symmetry 90–92
attitudes and planetary effects 106f
Au (vowel) 39
— and soul moods 52f
— and Sun 22
Aum 52
Ausländer, Rose 64–66, 85–88

B (consonant) 126
brain 104

Calendar of the Soul (Steiner) 33, 60–63, 81–85
Cancer 72f, 75, 77f, 92, 94

Capricorn 74f, 77f, 92, 94
centrifugal and centripetal gestures 23
circle dance 117f
colour gestures, archetypal 130
contemplation, deep (expression of Saturn) 19, 22, 25, 63, 66, 94
contraction and expansion 27, 32, 59f, 75, 81, 126, 128
counterimages 96f
creation, capacity for (expression of Moon) 16, 20, 22, 25, 62

daytime consciousness 120
Deventer, Erna Wolfram van 21
Domin, Hilde 65, 86

E (vowel) 40
— and Mars 21
— and metamorphosis of the I 50
— and soul moods 53
—, stages of manifestation 43f
ego, lower I 120
egotistic, self-centred nature (expression of Mercury) 16, 22, 24, 62, 65, 93
Ei (vowel) 39, 47f
— and Moon 22
— and soul moods 53f
Ephesus, initiates of 28
Ephesus verse (by Rudolf Steiner) 31, 34

etheric body 28–30, 56
—, 'cultural' 29f, 32
—, dual nature of 23
—, movement of 55
—, natural 29f, 32
exercises, first eurythmy 113–20
expansion and contraction 27, 32, 59f, 75, 81, 126, 128

Gemini 73, 75, 77f, 92, 94
Göbel, Thomas 28, 93
Greek sclupture 115
Guardian of the Threshold (by Rudolf Steiner) 88f, 118

Hallelujah 128
heart 102

I (self) 57, 120–32
—, breathing of 26, 120–22
—, dual nature of 24
—, exercises and meditations for the 125–32
—, higher 120
—, lower (ego) 120
—, manifestation in soul 24
—, modes of the 93–95
I (vowel) 39, 127
— and Mercury 22
— and metamorphosis of the I 49f
— and soul moods 52f
—, stages of manifestation 44f
IAO exercise 118f, 129, 131

Julius, Frits 110
Jupiter 47
— and wisdom 18, 21, 25, 61f, 66
—, colour triad 18
—, expression of *see* wisdom-imbued activity
— effects on human life 106–10
— gesture 18, 21, 40
—, life processes 101f
—, vowel of *see O* (vowel)

kidneys 103

L (consonant) 127f
Leo 72, 75–78, 90, 92–94
Libra 72, 75f, 78, 92, 94
Lievegoed, Bernard 101
life phases and planetary effects 105f
life processes, seven 28–32, 101–4
Lindenau, Christof 32
listening to speech dynamics 116
liver 102
loving, selfless nature (expression of Venus) 15, 22, 24, 61, 65
Lucifer 96
lungs 103

Maier-Smits, Lory 113
Mars 44, 102
—, colour triad 17
—, expression of *see* aggression, capacity for
— effects on human life 105–10
— gesture 17, 21, 39f
—, life processes 102
—, vowel of *see E* (vowel)
Mercury 45, 103
—, colour triad 16
— effects on human life 105–9
—, expression of *see* egotistic, self-centred nature
— gesture 16, 22, 39
—, life processes 103
—, vowel of *see I* (vowel)
Moon 28
—, colour triad 16
—, expression of *see* creation, capacity for
— effects on human life 105–7, 109
— gesture 16, 22, 39
—, life processes 103f
—, vowel of *see Ei* (vowel)

night-time consciousness 120

O (vowel) 40, 49
— and Jupiter 21
— and metamorphosis of the I 51
— and soul moods 53
—, stages of manifestation 46f

physical body, dual nature of 23
Pisces 36, 75, 77f, 92, 94
planetary sequence 34–37

Sagittarius 74f, 77f, 92, 94
Saturn 48
—, colour triad 19
—, expression of *see* contemplation, deep
— effects on human life 106f, 109f
— gesture 19, 22, 40
—, life processes 101
—, vowel of *see U* (vowel)
Scorpio 73, 75f, 78, 92, 94
sculpture, contemplating Greek 115
self-centred nature *see* egotistic, self-centred nature
soul, dual nature of 23
soul forms, twelve 93–95
sound to speech form 58f
speech dynamics, listening to 116
spiral, Euclidean 130
spiral, projective geometry 130
spleen 101
Steiner, Rudolf *passim*
—, *Calendar of the Soul* 33, 60–63, 81–85
—, Curative Education Course 120
—, Ephesus verse 31, 34
—, *Eurythmy as Visible Speech* 14, 23
—, *Eurythmy: its Birth and Development* 113
—, *Guardian of the Threshold* 88f, 118
—, *Twelve Moods* 35f, 95
stepping exercise 113f

Sun
—, colour triad 14
— effects on human life 105–9
—, expression of *see* whole human being
— gesture 14, 22, 38f
—, life processes 102
—, vowel of *see Au* (vowel)
symmetry and assymmetry 90–92

TAO meditation 131
Taurus 36, 73, 75, 77f, 92, 94

U (vowel) 40, 49
— and metamorphosis of the I 51
— and Saturn 22
— and soul moods 53
—, stages of manifestation 47f

Venus 43
—, colour triad 15
— effects on human life 105–9
—, expression of *see* loving, selfless nature
— gesture 15, 22, 39
—, life processes 103
—, vowel of *see A* (vowel)
Virgo 72, 75f, 78, 92, 94
vowels, response of etheric body 38–40

walking 79f
whole human being (expression of Sun) 14, 22, 24, 60, 64, 93f
wisdom-imbued activity (expression of Jupiter) 18f, 61, 66
Wolfram, Erna *see* Deventer, E
writing with feet (exercise) 117

zodiac gestures and astral body 71–75, 79

You may also be interested in...

The Zodiac Gestures in Eurythmy

Werner Barfod

'An absolute treasure-trove of information on the Zodiac... I would thoroughly recommend this book to anyone and consider it an absolute must-have for any eurythmist.'

– *Saraphir Qaa-Rishi, qualified eurythmist and teacher*

The zodiac, as representative of the whole cosmos, is a vital part of human spirituality, acting as the backdrop to human life. But it can be hard to fathom the zodiac's secrets, even through meditation. Werner Barfod draws a parallel between meditative exercises and eurythmy practice, and shows how zodiac gestures in eurythmy can reveal cosmic insights.

This is a book for eurythmy teachers and practitioners who want to deepen their art and spiritual work.

florisbooks.co.uk

For news on all our **latest books**,
and to receive **exclusive discounts**,
join our mailing list at:

florisbooks.co.uk

Plus subscribers get a FREE book
with every online order!

We will never pass your details to anyone else.

www.ingramcontent.com/pod-product-compliance
Lightning Source LLC
Chambersburg PA
CBHW061748070526
44585CB00025B/2832